EMOTIONAL INTELLIGENCE

People Smart Role Models

Emerson Klees

Cameo Press

Rochester, New York

For information, write:

Cameo Press
P. O. Box 18131
Rochester, New York 14618

Library of Congress Control Number 2011919696

ISBN 978-1-891046-14-8

Printed in the United States of America
9 8 7 6 5 4 3 2 1

Other Books by Emerson Klees

The Human Values Series

Role Models of Human Values

One Plus One Equals Three—Pairing Man / Woman Strengths: Role Models of Teamwork (1998)
Entrepreneurs in History—Success vs. Failure: Entrepreneurial Role Models (1999)
Staying With It: Role Models of Perseverance (1999)
The Drive to Succeed: Role Models of Motivation (2002)
The Will to Stay With It: Role Models of Determination (2002)
Paul Garrett: Dean of American Winemakers (2010)
A Song of the Vine: A Reflection on Life (2011)

The Moral Navigator

Inspiring Legends and Tales With a Moral I: Stories From Around the World (2007)
Inspiring Legends and Tales With a Moral II: Stories From Around the World (2007)
Inspiring Legends and Tales With a Moral III: Stories From Around the World (2007)

TABLE OF CONTENTS

PREFACE

The purpose of this book is to illustrate the importance of people skills in achieving success using role models from history. Being smart, if defined as having a high Intelligence Quotient (IQ), certainly contributes to achievement, but the Emotional Quotient (EQ), the measure of Emotional Intelligence, is a more important factor in being successful.

It has been determined that IQ contributes approximately 20% to success, leaving approximately 80% to other factors, such as EQ. Furthermore, the traits that make up Emotional Intelligence, including emotional control, empathy, and perseverance, are factors that can be improved, unlike IQ, which remains relatively fixed from young adulthood.

We all have acquaintances and friends who may not be the brightest or the most highly educated people that we know, but who have achieved success in life, perhaps notable success. They are probably doing what they want to be doing for a career and what they are good at doing. They may have accomplished their goals by recognizing their weaknesses and strengths and by working hard. It is likely that they have addressed their weaknesses by teaming up with a person or persons with complementary strengths.

The principal goal of this book is to aid the reader in understanding the elements of Emotional Intelligence, potentially allowing him or her to become more of a "people person." If we can identify our shortcomings, whether they are insufficient optimism, lack of assertiveness, poor motivation, or other factors, then we can strive to improve our EQ.

A debt is acknowledged to other authors for their work on the subject of Emotional Intelligence, particularly Daniel Goleman, Harvey Deutschendorf, and Mel Silberman.

PROLOGUE

"Emotional Intelligence refers to an array of attributes and tools that enables us to deal with the pressures and demands of our environment. Emotional Intelligence has been referred to as common sense or advanced common sense. Street smarts is another term that has been used in connection with Emotional Intelligence."

Harvey Deutschendorf, *The Other Kind of Smart*

A principal goal in life is to be happy. We may have wealth and many possessions, but if we aren't happy, what is it all worth? One of the key factors of happiness is success. If we are successful, we have a better chance of being happy. Nevertheless, being successful is not a guarantee of happiness.

We would like to know how to be successful at work and in our family relationships in order to have more satisfying and fulfilling lives. In addition to success with a career and at home, higher-level purposes exist: helping others and making the world a better place in which to live. Helping others contributes to our own happiness. Emotional Intelligence is a heavy contributor to our attainment of success and happiness.

According to Daniel Goleman in *Emotional Intelligence,* "[Some] subscribe to a narrow view of intelligence, arguing that IQ is a genetic given that cannot be changed by life experience, that our destiny is largely fixed by these aptitudes. That argument ignores the more challenging question: What can change that will help [us] fare better in life? What factors are at play, for example, when people of high IQ flounder and those of modest IQ do surprisingly well?

"The difference quite often lies in the abilities called Emotional Intelligence, which includes self-control, zeal, and persistence, and the ability to motivate oneself. And these skills . . . can be taught, giving [us] a better chance to use whatever intellectual potential the genetic lottery has given [us]."

Also according to Goleman, "Academic intelligence has little to do with emotional life. The brightest among us can flounder on the shoals of unbridled passions and unruly impulse; people with high IQs can be stunningly poor pilots of their private lives. One of psychology's open secrets is the relatively inability of grades, IQ, or SAT scores, despite their popular mystique, to predict unerringly who will succeed in life.

"To be sure, there is a relationship between IQ and life circumstances for large groups as a whole; many people with low IQs end up in menial jobs and those with high IQs tend to become well-paid—but by no means always. There are widespread exceptions to the rule that IQ predicts success—many (or more) exceptions than cases that fit the rule."

All of us know of people who dropped out of high school or who decided not to go to college who became very successful in life, perhaps as contractors or entrepreneurs. We probably also know individuals who were at the top of their class academically but who never really found their way in life.

The attributes of Emotional Intelligence, including motivation, leadership, negotiation / persuasion, and conflict resolution, are important in the workplace in many ways. Emotional Intelligence and productivity are directly related. Studies conducted in the workplace have indicated that from 27 to 45 percent of success on the job is determined by our Emotional Intelligence. In an organization, ability to work with others is of the utmost importance. People skills contribute heavily to working well with others. Being a "people person" is as important in the workplace as it is in life itself.

Many of the biographical sketches in this book are based on profiles in earlier Human Values Series books:

The Drive to Succeed: Role Models of Motivation
Entrepreneurs in History—Success vs. Failure: Entrepreneurial Role Models
Staying With It: Role Models of Perseverance
The Will to Stay With It: Role Models of Determination

These books have end notes and comprehensive bibliographies for further reading.

INTRODUCTION

"Emotional Intelligence refers to the capacity for recognizing our own feelings and those of others, for motivating ourselves, and for managing emotions well in ourselves and in our relationships. It describes abilities distinct from, but complementary to, academic intelligence, the purely cognitive capacities measured by IQ. Many people who are book smart but lack emotional intelligence end up working for people who have lower IQs than they but who excel in Emotional Intelligence skills."

Daniel Goleman, *Working with Emotional Intelligence*

Emotional Intelligence has been widely written about, with some variations in the attributes that make up EQ. In *Working with Emotional Intelligence,* author Daniel Goleman identified five basic emotional and social competencies:

- Self-awareness: Having a realistic assessment of our own abilities and a well-grounded sense of self-confidence
- Self-regulation: Handling our emotions so that they facilitate rather than interfere with the task at hand
- Motivation: Using our deepest preferences to move and guide us toward our goals
- Empathy: Sensing what people are feeling, being able to take their perspective
- Social skills: Handling emotions in relationships well and accurately reading social situations and networks; using these skills to persuade and lead, negotiate and settle disputes, for cooperation and teamwork

In *People Smart,* Mel Silberman identifies the skills involved in being people smart:

- Understanding people
- Expressing yourself clearly
- Asserting your needs
- Exchanging feedback
- Influencing others
- Resolving conflict
- Being a team player
- Shifting gears / flexibility

PART I

Role models in Part I of this book illustrate the following traits of Emotional Intelligence:

Perseverance
Empathy
Optimism
Persuasion / Negotiation
Leadership
Emotional Control
Social Responsibility
Motivation
Assertiveness
Relationships
Teamwork

Perseverance

Perseverance is a critical factor in accomplishment and success. Intelligence alone doesn't guarantee success. Many brilliant men and women in history didn't gain the same distinction as their peers with less intelligence who worked hard and persevered. Frequently, an individual with superior perseverance and average intelligence outperforms one with superior intelligence and average or below average perseverance. As David G. Ryans observes in "The Meaning of Persistence" in the *Journal of General Psychology*: "Persistence and success are inseparably bound together in the popular mind, and rightly so. For achievement through aptitude or ability alone is undoubtedly the exception rather than the rule. Most tasks demand more than brilliance."

Empathy

In *The Other Kind of Smart,* Harvey Deutschendorf observes: "Empathy means being able to accurately read where other people are at emotionally. It means being able to get below the words others are saying to sense the underlying feelings. To do that, we must be able to pick up not only the words but also the force and tone with which they are said. Along with this, we need to take into account facial expression, posture, and other indicators that will give us valuable clues into the person's emotional state." Empathy should not be confused with sympathy, which brings out our own feelings as opposed to reading the feelings of others.

Optimism

Daniel Goleman in *Emotional Intelligence* notes: "Optimism, like hope, means having a strong expectation that, in general, things will turn out all right, despite setbacks and frustrations. From the standpoint of Emotional Intelligence, optimism is an attitude that buffers people against falling into apathy, hopelessness, or depression in the face of tough going. And, as with hope, its near cousin, optimism pays dividends in life (providing of course it is realistic optimism)."

Persuasion / Negotiation

In *People Smart,* Mel Silberman observes: "Influencing others has to do with getting them to be receptive to your views, advice and recommendations. It is not about your getting them to admit that you are right or forcing them to do as you wish. You can't make someone see the world as you see it, but you can sometimes open their mind to new attitudes and effective courses of action. Unfortunately, many people are intent on making people over in their own image."

Leadership

Leadership is not the art of dominating people but that of persuading them to work toward common goals. In *The Other Kind of Smart,* Harvey Deutschendorf notes: "When employee satisfaction levels within organizations have been studied, dissatisfaction with leadership has come out as the most common reason for leaving the workplace. Leaders have a tremendous ability to influence the staff under them in both positive and negative ways. Effective leaders are able to use their people skills to encourage, motivate, and get the most from their employees, while ineffective ones can cause morale and productivity to plummet."

Emotional Control

According to Daniel Goleman in *Emotional Intelligence,* "Handling feelings so they are appropriate is an ability that builds on self-awareness . . . recognizing a feeling as it happens—the keystone of emotional intelligence—the ability to monitor feelings from moment to moment is crucial to psychological insight and and self-understanding. . . . [Managing emotions involves] the capacity to soothe oneself, to shake off rampant anxiety, gloom, or irritability. . . . People who are poor in this ability are constantly battling feelings of distress, while those who excel in it can bounce back far more quickly from life's setbacks and upsets."

Social Responsibility

In *The Other Kind of Smart,* Harvey Deutschendorf notes: "We are all socially responsible to the degree that we see ourselves as being part of something larger than ourselves. Socially responsible people have a sense of duty to make the world a better place in which to live . . . work that helps others brings us satisfaction and happiness. [A national opinion survey] has found that the people who reported the highest level of happiness and satisfaction were those that had jobs serving other people. The benefits of helping others are enormous."

Motivation

Abraham Maslow, who describes his theory of motivation in *Motivation and Personality,* outlines a hierarchy of needs in which people are concerned with needs at a higher level only when those at a lower level have been satisfied. The lowest level is the fulfillment of physiological needs, such as those for physical survival—food, drink, and shelter. The second level comprises safety needs, such as security, stability, protection, and freedom from anxiety and fear. Next are belongingness and love needs, topped by esteem needs.

Esteem needs, including those for self-esteem, self-respect, and the esteem of others, are divided into two categories. The first category involves the way that we see ourselves, such as the desire for strength, achievement, mastery, independence, and freedom. The second category concerns the way others see us, including status, fame, dominance, recognition, and appreciation. Maslow describes the need for self-actualization when all of the lower level needs are met:

> Even if all these needs are satisfied, we may still often (if not always) expect that a new discontent and restlessness will soon develop, unless the individual is doing what he, individually, is fitted for. A musician must make music, an artist must paint, a poet must write, if he is to be ultimately at peace with himself. What a man can be, he must be. He must be true to his own nature. This need we may call self-actualization. . . .

> It refers to a man's desire for self-fulfillment, namely, the tendency for him to become actualized in what he is potentially. This tendency might be phrased as the desire to become more and more what one idiosyncratically is, to become everything that one is capable of becoming.
>
> The specific form that these needs will take of course varies greatly from person to person. In one person it may take the form of the desire to be an ideal mother, in another it may be expressed athletically, and in still another it may be expressed in painting pictures or in inventions.

Assertiveness

In *The Other Kind of Smart,* Harvey Deutschendorf notes: "Healthy assertive people, while being clear about their wishes, respect the rights of others. As much as assertive people maintain their boundaries, they respect the boundaries of others. Assertiveness allows for a difference of opinion without an attempt to beat the other person into submission or force them to come around to another way of thinking. It allows a win-win situation, something that aggression does not. It is possible for two quite assertive people to maintain a close friendship and respect one another while disagreeing with each other."

Relationships

According to Daniel Goleman in *Emotional Intelligence,* "Improving one's Emotional Intelligence involves, in handling relationships:

- Increased ability to analyze and understand relationships
- Better at resolving conflicts and negotiating agreements
- Better at solving problems in relationships
- More assertive and skilled at communicating
- More popular and outgoing, friendly and involved with peers
- More sought out by peers
- More concerned and considerate
- More pro-social and harmonious in groups

- More sharing, cooperation, and helpfulness
- More democratic in dealing with others"

Teamwork

Mel Silberman discusses teamwork in *People Smart:* "A person's ability to be interpersonally intelligent is really challenged when it comes to teamwork. All of us are involved in some kind of teamwork, whether at work, with another parent, in a neighborhood group, or in a service organization. Being part of a team is challenging because you have less personal control over the outcome than you might have in a one-on-one relationship. It's often frustrating because you have fewer opportunities to get your point across and persuade others. Working as a team takes special skills, such as complementing the styles of others, coordinating the efforts of team members without bossing them around, and building consensus."

PART II

Role Models in Part II illustrate five examples of failure vs. success, along with a description of the environments in which they strived, the factors that contributed to their success or failure (or limited success), and the contribution of their Emotional Intelligence traits.

- Invention of the Steamboat—
  John Fitch and Robert Fulton

- Invention of the Telephone—
  Philipp Reis and Alexander Graham Bell

- Vulcanization Development—
  Charles Goodyear and Thomas Hancock

- Invention of the Sewing Machine—
  Elias Howe and Isaac Singer

- Invention of the Airplane—
  Samuel Langley and the Wright Brothers

PART I

ROLE MODELS OF EMOTIONAL INTELLIGENCE

Perseverance

Empathy

Optimism

Persuasion / Negotiation

Leadership

Emotional Control

Social Responsibility

Motivation

Assertiveness

Relationships

Teamwork

"The term 'Emotional Intelligence' is used . . . to encompass an incisive, broad and diverse approach in describing . . . closely related terms. . . . They tend to focus on the following competencies:

- The ability to recognize and understand emotions and to express feelings non-destructively
- The ability to understand how others feel and relate with them cooperatively
- The ability to manage and control emotions effectively
- The ability to manage change and the emotions generated by change, and to adapt and solve problems of a personal and interpersonal nature
- The ability to generate positive affect and be self-motivated"

Reuven Bar-On, J. G. Maree, and Maurice Jesse Elias, editors, *Educating People to Be Emotionally Intelligent*

A purpose of Part I is to provide role models of Emotional Intelligence from history to illustrate the traits that make up the Emotional Quotient (EQ). According to author Samuel Smiles, "Example teaches better than precept. It is the best modeler of the character of men and women. To set a lofty example is the richest bequest a man [or woman] can leave behind."

All of these role models had a high EQ and a number of them are assumed to have had a high IQ as well. Also, they all had the Emotional Intelligence traits of perseverance, optimism, and motivation. In addition, since they were all achievers, they had other EQ traits that varied from individual to individual as well as additional positive traits, such as determination and resilience.

The examples provided are not an all-inclusive list of the traits of Emotional Intelligence. Others include independence, an aptitude for problem solving, and flexibility. We can learn from these role models to aid in increasing our own Emotional Intelligence.

CHAPTER 1

PERSEVERANCE—ROLE MODELS

Thomas Edison (1847-1931) Inventor Extraordinaire

Marie Curie (1867-1934) Discoverer of Radium

"Nothing in the world can take the place of persistence.

Talent will not; nothing is more common than unsuccessful men with talent.

Genius will not; unrewarded genius is almost a proverb.

Education alone will not; the world is full of educated derelicts.

Persistence and determination alone are omnipotent."

Calvin Coolidge

(Appeared on the cover of the program for his memorial service in 1933)

THOMAS EDISON—Inventor Extraordinaire

"Genius is one percent inspiration and 99 percent perspiration." For example, "From 18 to 20 hours a day for the last seven months, I have worked on the single word 'specia.' I said to the phonograph, 'specia, specia, specia,' but the instrument replied 'pecia, pecia, pecia.' It was enough to drive one mad. But I held firm, and I have succeeded."

Thomas Edison

Thomas Edison was a persevering individual throughout his career as an inventor. He conducted thousands of experiments in which he considered many alternatives until he found one that suited his needs. Even if he had not found the material or approach that he was seeking, he was eliminating alternatives that would not work well or were not practical. Of many examples of Edison's perseverance, two notable ones are his efforts to perfect the phonograph and his struggle to find a practical filament for the lightbulb.

While attempting to improve the transmitter used with Alexander Graham Bell's telephone, Edison had his first thoughts about inventing a device for recording the human voice. His challenge was to find a material to improve the operation of the transmitter used to transmit voice over telephone lines. He tried hundreds of materials before arriving at the choice of carbon as the optimum transmitter material.

Edison made a sketch of a device that he felt could be used to record and play back the sound of the human voice. He asked one of his associates to make a model from the sketch. The device consisted of a long, narrow cylinder on a shaft that was turned by a hand crank. A thin metal disk picked up the voice sound waves. Turning the crank caused the cylinder to rotate and a pin to move along the axis of the cylinder.

A pin in the center of the disk made a groove that modeled the voice pattern on tinfoil wrapped around the cylinder. Another pin used with a second disk picked up the voice pattern and converted it into vibrations that generated the sound. The quality of sound that this first phonograph reproduced was poor. However, Edison had proved that the voice could be recorded and then played back. He set this invention aside and worked on other projects.

Ten years later, Edison decided that he should do something to improve the fidelity of the sound of his phonograph. Its principal shortcomings were in reproducing the sibilants (hissing sounds) and the higher tones of musical notes. Edison noted that, in order to overcome the defects in his phonograph design, "I worked over one year, 20 hours a day, Sundays and all, to get the word 'specia' perfectly recorded and reproduced on the phonograph. When this was done, I knew everything else could be done."

A second example of Edison's perseverance was his search for a practical filament material for the electric lightbulb. Electric light had been around for a long time. The first electric arc light had been developed by the English scientist, Sir Humphrey Davy, and had been improved upon by Paul Jablochkoff, a Russian engineer. However, their arc lights generated a very glaring light and radiated considerable heat. The initial arc lamp burned for only a few minutes before the filament burned out. Improvements had been made that allowed the filament to last several hours.

Edison's challenge was to find a filament material that would heat up from the low currents and high voltages used at the time. Filaments burned out quickly when in contact with oxygen. He had to find a way to minimize the amount of oxygen in contact with the filament. In his search for a filament material, he needed a substance with a high melting point that would last considerably longer than a few hours.

The first material that Edison tried was carbon. His first carbon filaments were carbonized strips of paper. These filaments burned out in eight minutes. His next series of experiments were with threads of rare metals. He tried barium, platinum, rhodium, ruthenium, titanium, and zirconium.

Of these materials, platinum worked the best. He used a double spiral of platinum for his filament. Next he investigated the problem of minimizing the amount of oxygen in contact with the filament. He asked his glass blower to make some enclosed, pear-shaped bulbs.

The platinum filament provided five times more footcandles of light than previous experiments. However, platinum was a rare metal and was expensive. He considered using tungsten, the material used in lightbulbs later, but, unfortunately, he did not have the delicate tools required to work with it.

Edison persisted in his search for an improved filament. He experimented with various grasses, linen thread, and wood splinters. He even tried a red hair from a man's beard. His goal was to make a light bulb for 50 cents or less. He had moderate success in an experiment with a bamboo filament. Edison tried over 1,600 different materials in his search for an optimum material for his filament.

On October 21, 1879, Edison used a filament made of carbonized thread. In that experiment, the light bulb burned for 13 1/2 hours. The next day he used a different type of cotton thread, which had also been carbonized. That filament burned for 40 hours. Edison and his assistants were jubilant. If they could make a filament that would burn for 40 hours, they could make one that would last for a multiple of 40 hours.

Later, Edison was able to make a filament by carbonizing a thread of cellulose extruded from a die. This filament burned longer than the carbonized cotton filament. Also, he found that he could make a filament from carbonized cardboard that would burn for 160 hours.

On New Year's Eve 1879, 3,000 people came to Edison's laboratory in Menlo Park, New Jersey, to witness their first view of Edison's incandescent light and to celebrate with him. The age of electric light had begun.

MARIE CURIE —Discoverer of Radium

"Life is not easy for any of us. But what of that? We must have perseverance and above all have confidence in ourselves. We must believe that we are gifted for something, and that this thing, at whatever costs, must be attained."

Marie Curie

Marie Sklodwska left her native Poland and moved to Paris in 1891 to study at the Sorbonne because women weren't permitted to study at the university level in Poland. She graduated first in her class with a master's degree in physics and realized that mathematics was important to her career, so she studied for a second master's degree. Within a year, she graduated second in her class with a master's degree in mathematics.

In 1894, Curie was asked by the Society for the Encouragement of National Industry to prepare a paper on the magnetic properties of various kinds of steel. Her laboratory at the Sorbonne wasn't adequate for the assignment. She was introduced to the laboratory head of the School of Chemistry and Physics of the University of Paris, which had the necessary facilities. The head of the laboratory was 35-year-old Pierre Curie, who was already a physicist distinguished for his pioneering work on the symmetry of crystals. On July 26, 1895, after a ten-month courtship, they were married in a civil ceremony.

In August 1896, Curie was first in her class in her final examinations for a teaching certificate. She decided to study for a doctorate in science. Other women had attempted to earn this degree, but none had yet been successful. Curie would be a pioneer in her next academic effort, and she was acutely aware that she would have to compete with men on their terms. She would have to overcome considerable male prejudice, but she didn't hesitate to undertake the challenge. Curie would have to do original work of substance, such as solving a previously unsolved problem or discovering something that would add to the world's knowledge. The topic for her dissertation grew out of work by Henri Becquerel, who investigated whether X-rays were related to the property of fluorescence that causes some crystals to emit electromagnetic radiation, especially of visible light after being exposed to light.

Becquerel exposed fluorescent materials to sunlight and then placed them adjacent to a photographic plate covered with black paper. The first material he tested that would fog the photographic plate was a uranium compound (uranium salts). He found that the plates wrapped with black paper became fogged even if the uranium salts weren't exposed to sunlight. The emitted rays were spontaneous emissions inherent to the crystals themselves. Becquerel determined that these emanations came from all uranium compounds.

Curie's goal for her dissertation was to discover the source of these emitted rays. She had to find a laboratory in which to work. Neither she nor Pierre had sufficient lab space, and they couldn't afford to rent a lab for this purpose. Curie was given an unused storeroom on the grounds of the School of Physics. It was a rough wooden shed with a leaky glass roof and no electricity or heat. In the winter, the temperature inside her makeshift laboratory dropped to 42 degrees Fahrenheit, which caused her to question some of her results. She had to beg and borrow instruments to equip her laboratory.

Curie's early results indicated that the strength of the emitted rays was directly proportional to the quantity of uranium in her sample. She could heat the sample, expose it to light, or combine it with other chemicals, but the intensity of the rays remained constant. She concluded that this radiation she was encountering must be a property of the atom of the substance. This critical hypothesis led to the further investigation of the structure of atoms. She found that thorium as well as uranium indicated radioactivity on her electrometer.

Marie asked Pierre to provide her with samples containing uranium and thorium from the School of Physics. She was surprised to find that three of the samples that Pierre had provided, chalcocite, pitchblende, and uranite, indicated considerably greater radioactivity than the amounts of uranium and thorium in the samples warranted. She repeatedly retested her results. She concluded that there was another radioactive element in the samples in addition to uranium and thorium. It was an element of considerable strength and seemed to have the greatest intensity in pitchblende, an ore of uranium.

In April 1898, Curie announced to the Academy of Science the probable existence of a powerful new element in pitchblende. Her next challenge was to isolate the element, refine it to a pure a substance, and determine its atomic weight. Pierre set aside his other projects to work with his wife in the laboratory.

Marie and Pierre ground the pitchblende ore into smaller particles, boiled it with acids and other chemicals, filtered it, tested both the slush and the residue, and discarded the portion that indicated no radioactivity. Then they repeated the process in an attempt to break down the ore into its component elements. At the conclusion of the process, they found rays emanating from two residual elements, not just one. They announced the existence of a new element similar to bismuth that was 400 times more radioactive than uranium. They named it polonium, after the ancient name for Poland, Polonia.

In December 1898, the Curies announced the discovery of radium. In 1902, after working almost four years reducing six tons of pitchblende to its component elements, they had one tenth of a gram of gray-white powder. Radium has some of the chemical properties of barium, and the intensity of its radioactivity is 900 times that of uranium.

Marie and Pierre were confronted with a significant obstacle to further work in the laboratory. They didn't have the funds to obtain the large quantities of pitchblende that were required for future experiments. Radium was present in less than one part per million in pitchblende. They obtained several tons of waste pitchblende. Since the uranium had already been extracted for industrial uses, it made their research easier, and, because the pitchblende was waste, they obtained it by paying only transportation costs.

The Curies worked in primitive conditions, and their work required long hours of hard, physical labor. A distinguished German chemist observed, "At my urgent request the Curie laboratory, in which radium was discovered a short time ago, was shown to me . . . It was a cross between a stable and a potato-cellar, and, if I had not seen the worktable with the chemical apparatus, I would have thought it a practical joke."

The working conditions were considered by the two highly motivated people to be secondary to the content of the work. Curie's viewpoint was "It was in this miserable old shed that the best and happiest years of our life were spent entirely consecrated to our work. I sometimes passed the whole day stirring a mass in ebullition, with an iron rod nearly as big as myself. In the evening I was broken with fatigue."

The Curies found that radium could cause bad burns, but that it could also retard the growth of tumors, destroy infected cells, and arrest some types of cancer. Curie graduated from the University of Paris with the degree of Doctor of Physical Science "tres honorable."

In 1903, Marie and Pierre shared the Nobel Prize in physics with Henri Becquerel for their pioneering work in radioactivity. Their happy, fulfilled life together didn't continue for long, however. On April 19, 1906, Pierre was run over and killed by a horse-drawn carriage. Curie was devastated. She was 40 years old and faced the decision of what to do with her future. She decided to continue their work alone. As a team, their individual strengths had complemented each other. Pierre contributed many of the original ideas and unusual viewpoints to a problem, but it was Curie with her dogged persistence who implemented Pierre's theories and carried them to a meaningful conclusion.

In 1911, Curie was nominated again for the Nobel Prize for work done since Pierre's death. It was the first time that anyone had received a second Nobel Prize. The Sorbonne and the Pasteur Institute established a dual laboratory, one in Curie's name for her work in radioactivity and one in Pasteur's name for biological research. The "Institute of Radium: Pavilion Curie" was opened in 1914. In 1925, she traveled to Warsaw to lay the cornerstone of another research facility, the Radium Institute of Warsaw.

Initially, the Curies weren't aware of many of the dangerous effects of working with radioactive materials. In her middle age, Curie became increasingly aware of the risks to her, personally, in working with these substances. She persevered with her research, but realized that some of her physical problems were due to her long-term exposure. She worked in the laboratory until May 1934, when a fever caused her to leave. She was diagnosed with bronchitis and exhaustion and died in July 1934 of pernicious anemia.

* * *

Edison and Curie had many personal strengths, including motivation and determination; however, they are outstanding examples of perseverance. Marie and Pierre Curie are also an excellent example of teamwork.

CHAPTER 2

EMPATHY—ROLE MODELS

Florence Nightingale (1820-1910) Nursing and Medical Pioneer

Clara Barton (1821-1912) Founder of the American Red Cross

"The ability to see the world from another person's perspective, the capacity to tune into what someone else might be thinking and feeling about a situation—regardless of how that view might differ from your own perception . . . is an extremely strong interpersonal tool. When you make an empathetic statement, even in the midst of an otherwise tense or antagonistic encounter, you shift the balance. A contentious and uneasy interchange becomes a more collaborative alliance."

Steven J. Stein and Howard E. Book, *The EQ Edge*

FLORENCE NIGHTINGALE—Nursing and Medical Pioneer

"It was not by gentle sweetness and womanly self-abnegation that she had brought order out of chaos in the Scutari Hospitals, that, from her own resources, she had clothed the British Army, that she spread her dominion over the serried and reluctant powers of the official world; it was by strict method, by stern discipline, by rigid attention to detail, by ceaseless labor, by the fixed determination of an indomitable will."

Lytton Strachey, *Eminent Victorians*

Florence Nightingale is known principally for her work at military hospitals during the Crimean War. However, her contributions were much greater than that. She was the driving force in the reform of British Army medical services during and after the Crimean War in designing hospitals with the patient in mind, in the establishment of a school of nursing with higher standards than previous ones, and in the administration of medical services for the army in India.

This effort involved guiding those in positions of power in the British government, choosing chairmen for key committees, and generally steering medical and hospital reform, both military and civilian, for over 40 years. Nightingale provided direction for the careers of many Members of Parliament and advice to every Viceroy of India before he left England to assume his new duties.

Virtually all of Nightingale's girlhood friends were contented to become wives, mothers, and hostesses whose principal interests in life were social activities. She herself was bored with the social whirl and felt obliged to do something meaningful with her life. She viewed this as a call and entered this note in her diary: "On February 7, 1837, God spoke to me and called me to His service."

However, Nightingale did not know what form this service was going to take; she knew that it was going to have something to do with ministering to the sufferings of humanity. It did not become clear to her for seven years that her call was caring for the sick.

In the fall of 1842, while visiting the Baroness and Baron von Bunsen, the Prussian Ambassador to Great Britain, Nightingale asked them what a person could do to relieve the suffering of those who cannot help themselves. The Baron told her about the work at Kaiserswerth, Germany, where Protestant deaconesses were trained in the institution's hospital to nurse the poor who were sick. Nightingale had not considered nursing as a way of serving those in need, and she did not follow up on this suggestion at the time.

By the spring of 1844, however, Nightingale was certain that her life's work was with the sick in hospitals. Thirteen years later she wrote, "Since I was 24 . . . there never was any vagueness in my plans or ideas as to what God's work was for me."

In June 1844, Dr. Ward Howe, the American philanthropist, visited the Nightingales at Embley. Nightingale asked Dr. Howe: "Do you think it would be unsuitable and unbecoming for a young Englishwoman to devote herself to works of charity in hospitals and elsewhere as Catholic sisters do?" Dr. Howe replied: "My dear Miss Florence, it would be unusual, and in England whatever is unusual is thought to be unsuitable; but I say to you 'go forward.' If you have a vocation for that way of life, act up to your inspiration and you will find there is never anything unbecoming or unladylike in doing your duty for the good of others. Choose, go on with it, wherever it may lead you and God be with you."

Nightingale considered how to present to her parents her plan to spend three months in nursing training at nearby Salisbury Infirmary, where the head physician was Dr. Fowler, a family friend. She broached the subject with her parents in December 1845, during a visit by Dr. Fowler and his wife.

The Nightingales were strongly opposed and could not understand why Florence wanted to "disgrace herself." She wrote later: "It was as if I had wanted to be a kitchen-maid."

Nightingale was distressed because she knew what she had to do, but she was prevented from doing it. Lytton Strachey, in *Eminent Victorians,* observed: "A weaker spirit would have been overwhelmed by the load of such distresses—would have yielded or snapped. But this extraordinary young woman held firm and fought her way to victory. With an amazing persistency, during the eight years that followed her rebuff over Salisbury Hospital, she struggled and worked and planned."

While continuing to perform her social obligations, Nightingale studied hospital reports and public health material. She built up a detailed knowledge of sanitary conditions that ultimately allowed her to become the foremost expert in England and on the Continent in her subject.

Finally, Nightingale was given the opportunity to receive nursing training at Kaiserswerth. Her spartan life started at five o'clock in the morning and the work was hard; but, in her words, "I find the deepest interest in everything here and am so well in body and mind. This is life. Now I know what it is to live and to love life, and I really should be sorry to leave life. . . . I wish for no other earth, no other world than this."

Nightingale met Dr. Elizabeth Blackwell, the first woman medical doctor in modern times, in the spring of 1851 in London, where Blackwell had come for further medical training. Nightingale talked with Blackwell about the strength of her commitment to hospital nursing.

In April 1853, Nightingale heard of an opportunity that suited her parents' requirements. The Institution for the Care of Sick Gentlewomen in Distressed Circumstances had encountered problems and was to be reorganized and moved to another location. Nightingale took charge and was responsible not only for the management of the institution but also its finances.

Nightingale had one year of nursing experience in March 1854, when England and France declared war on Russia. In June, the British Army landed at Varna on the Black Sea. When they embarked from Varna for the Crimea there was a shortage of transport ships, so they had to leave hospital tents and regimental medicine chests behind. On September 30, the British and the French defeated the Russians in the Battle of the Alma with heavy casualties on both sides.

British casualties did not receive proper care, since there were no litters or hospital wagons to transport them to a site to receive medical attention. When the wounded were carried by their comrades to receive the care of a doctor, no bandages or splints were available, nor were there any anesthetics or painkillers.

William Russell's dispatches to the *London Times* brought the conditions of the casualties to the attention of the British public. Two weeks after the Battle of the Alma, he wrote, "It is with feelings of surprise and anger that the public will learn that no sufficient preparations have been made for the care of the wounded. Not only are there not sufficient surgeons . . . not only are there no dressers and nurses . . . there is not even linen to make bandages."

Russell visited the French Army to see how their wounded were being treated. He found that their medical facilities and nursing care were excellent, and that 50 Sisters of Charity had accompanied their army. In another article to his newspaper, he asked, “Why have we no Sisters of Charity? There are numbers of able-bodied and tender-hearted English women who would joyfully and with alacrity go out to devote themselves to nursing the sick and wounded, if they could be associated for that purpose and placed under proper protection.”

The Secretary for War during the Crimean War was Sidney Herbert, a good friend of Nightingale and her family. He wrote to ask if she would go to the Crimea to organize and superintend the nurses to care for the wounded.

Nightingale immediately began interviewing candidates and ultimately selected 14 nurses who, along with 10 Catholic Sisters and 14 Anglican Sisters, accompanied her to Scutari. She was appointed Superintendent of the Female Nursing Establishment of the English General Hospitals in Turkey. This title caused her problems, since it was construed to restrict her authority to Turkey and to exclude her from the Crimea in Russia.

Nightingale arrived at the military hospital in Scutari on November 4, 1854, 10 days after the Battle of Balaclava, where the Light Brigade was decimated by pitting cavalry against artillery, and 10 days before the Battle of Inkerman. She encountered a medical support system in total collapse, due to insufficient planning, poor execution of the few plans that did exist, and generally inadequate administration hampered by bureaucratic constrictions.

The Commissariat was responsible for the procurement, financing, transporting, and warehousing of hospital supplies. The Purveyor was responsible for food for the sick but did not procure it; the Commissariat did, and the organizations did not work well together.

Barrack Hospital, with four miles of beds, was not big enough. Nightingale had to plan, equip, and finance accommodations for 800 additional patients when the casualties from the Battles of Balaclava and Inkerman began to arrive. Open sewers, which ran under Barrack Hospital, were filled with lice, rats, and other vermin. Ventilation was poor and the stench was horrible. Working in these conditions is an indication of the strength of Nightingale’s empathy for her patients. She became a purveyor of hospital supplies and a supplier of clothing to the patients.

Finances available to Nightingale were money sent to her from private sources in England and funds collected by the *London Times* for aid to the sick and the wounded. An eyewitness wrote, "I cannot conceive, as I now look back on the first three weeks after the arrival of the wounded from Inkerman, how it would have been possible to have avoided a state of things too disastrous to contemplate had not Miss Nightingale been there, with the aid of the means placed at her disposal."

Although Nightingale complied with regulations, her active style offended Dr. John Hall, Chief of the Medical Staff of the British Expeditionary Army. He found ways to obstruct her efforts. In particular, he was initially able to prevent her from supporting the two large hospitals in the Crimea by a strict interpretation of her title, Superintendent of the Female Nursing Establishment in *Turkey*. He claimed that her responsibility did not extend to the Crimea.

Coworkers were in awe of Nightingale. Dr. Sutherland said, "She is the mainspring of the work. Nobody who has not worked with her daily could know her, could have an idea of her strength and clearness of mind, her extraordinary powers joined with her benevolence of spirit. She is one of the most gifted creatures God ever made."

Nightingale worked incredibly long hours and gave personal attention to the patients, even those with infectious diseases. The administrative load was overwhelming, and she had no secretary to share the paperwork burden. By spring 1855, she was physically exhausted. Nightingale was becoming a legend in England. She received a letter from the Queen:

> You are, I know, well aware of the high sense I entertain of the Christian devotion which you have displayed during this great and bloody war, and I need hardly repeat to you how warm my admiration is for your services, which are fully equal to those of my dear and brave soldiers, whose sufferings you have had the privilege of alleviating in so merciful a manner.

In August 1856, Nightingale returned home from Scutari. Within a few weeks of her return, she visited the Queen and the Prince Consort at Balmoral Castle and made an excellent impression. The Prince wrote in his diary, "She put before us all the defects of our present military hospital system and the reforms that are needed." The Queen observed, "Such a head! I wish we had her at the War Office."

Nightingale became an influential person, and she knew how to use that influence. She negotiated Sidney Herbert's appointment as chairman of a royal commission whose function was to report on the health of the army.

During six months of extremely hard work, Nightingale assembled and wrote in her own hand "Notes Affecting the Health, Efficiency, and Hospital Administration of the British Army." This comprehensive 800-page document contained far-sighted recommendations for reform in the areas of hospital architecture, military medical requirements, sanitation, and medical statistics.

In December 1859, Nightingale published a nursing guide, *Notes on Nursing*. In 1860, she opened the Nightingale Training School for Nurses at St. Thomas Hospital and became known as the founder of modern nursing. She did this concurrently with her ongoing efforts for medical and sanitary reform, which continued for over 40 years. Administration was her strength; she established a cost accounting system for the Army Medical Services between 1860 and 1865 that was was still in use over 80 years later.

In November 1907, King Edward VII bestowed the Order of Merit on Nightingale, the first such award given to a woman. She died on August 13, 1910, after serving others for virtually her entire adult life.

During the time when Nightingale was pleading unsuccessfully with her parents to allow her to undertake nursing training, her mother confided her concerns to her friends. As noted by Lytton Strachey in *Eminent Victorians,* "At times, indeed, among her intimates, Mrs. Nightingale almost wept. 'We are ducks,' she said with tears in her eyes, 'who have hatched a wild swan.' But the poor lady was wrong; it was not a swan that they had hatched; it was an eagle."

CLARA BARTON—Founder of the American Red Cross

"A tremendous humanitarian . . . she nevertheless defied the usual way of doing things when it presented obstacles instead of solutions. She brought to her work not only a rare gift for organization but a persistence and determination that could overcome any obstacle in her path. The life of a person with vision is often one of struggle, of constantly fighting the status quo. Barton's life was filled with her battles for progress. She was one of the first . . . to realize that nursing must be done at the battlefront and that female nurses could be employed to do it. She was one of the first in her country to comprehend the importance of having the Red Cross in the United States. . . . She may have been the first person to realize the the International Red Cross could be used to aid people in times of peace."

Leni Hamilton, *Clara Barton*

Clara Barton, founder of the American Red Cross, was the youngest of five children. Clara's favorite brother was David. In July 1832, she saw David fall feet-first from the ridge post of a barn onto a pile of timber in the cellar. He developed a chronic headache, and, as the summer progressed, he contracted a fever.

Ten-year-old Clara became her brother's nurse. In her words, "From the first days and nights of his illness, I remained near his side. I could not be taken away from him, except by compulsion, and he was unhappy until my return. I learned to take all the directions for his medicines from his physicians . . . and to administer them like a genuine nurse. . . . thus it came about that I was the accepted and acknowledged nurse of a man almost too ill to recover."

Two doctors told the Bartons that their son's condition was hopeless. Clara cheered him up, fed him, bathed him, and read to him. She rarely left his side for two years. Finally, a new doctor, who was a believer in "hydrotherapy," examined David. He moved the young man to his sanatorium and began water therapy. David returned home in three weeks and was fully recovered in six weeks. He owed his life to his little sister, who gave him constant care and the will to live long enough to be cured.

Barton had many relatives who were teachers, and, at the age of 17, she passed an oral examination and began to teach school. She was an excellent teacher and was known for her discipline. After teaching for 12 years, she enrolled at the Clinton Liberal Institute to further her education. Upon completion of the program, she accepted a teaching position in Bordentown, New Jersey.

At the outbreak of the Civil War, Barton volunteered to help at the Washington Infirmary. She heard that the 6th Massachusetts regiment from Worchester had been attacked by a mob of Confederate sympathizers while traveling through Baltimore. Four men were killed, dozens were wounded, and all their baggage was stolen. They were dressed in winter uniforms and woolen underwear unsuitable for the spring and summer weather in Washington.

Using her own money, Barton furnished the men with summer underwear, eating utensils, food, pots, and pans, as well as handkerchiefs, needles, soap, thread, and towels. She advertised in the *Worchester Spy*, their hometown newspaper, that she would receive and distribute provisions for area servicemen. She received so many items that she had to ask the army quartermaster to warehouse them.

Barton heard that little medical care had been provided to the wounded after the disastrous First Battle of Bull Run. The wounded weren't treated, and they were left without food and water. She offered her services as a nurse, but encountered resistance. In the 1860s, women weren't considered strong enough to deal with conditions at the front. Propriety was also an issue. Finally, she received the long-awaited permission from Dr. William Hammond, Surgeon-General of the U. S.: "Miss C. H. Barton has permission to go upon the sick transports in any direction—for the purpose of distributing comforts for the sick and wounded—of nursing them, always subject to the direction of the surgeon in charge."

Barton was introduced to battlefield nursing at the Battle of Cedar Run in Virginia. She arrived with a wagon load of supplies just as brigade surgeon James Dunn was considering how to treat the wounded without supplies. He called her the "Angel of the Battlefield," a name that stayed with her. Her second battlefield service was treating the staggering casualties of the Second Battle of Bull Run in August 1862.

At the Battle of Chantilly, Barton had three sleepless nights in a row; she slept for two hours on the fourth night lying in water from the heavy rains. Returning to Washington, the train carrying the wounded was almost captured by the Confederate cavalry, who burned the station from which they had just departed.

At Antietam, when Barton arrived with supplies that were vitally needed, brigade surgeon Dunn was using corn husks for bandages. While she was giving a drink of water to a wounded soldier, a bullet passed through her sleeve, and the soldier fell back dead. Another soldier asked her to use his pocket knife to remove a musket ball from his cheek; he couldn't wait for the surgeon. With a sergeant holding the soldier's head, she removed the ball. These are examples of Barton's hands-on empathy for her patients.

In 1864, Barton was Superintendent of Nurses for General Benjamin Butler's Army of the James. She organized hospitals and their staffs and supervised their administration. After the war, Barton collected information on soldiers who were missing in action. As with her nursing jobs, she worked without pay. She located over 22,000 missing soldiers; eventually, she was paid for her efforts. She went to Europe to rest and stayed with friends in Switzerland.

Dr. Louis Appia of the Red Cross visited Barton. He asked why the United States had rejected his offer three times to join the Red Cross. Barton had not heard of the organization founded by Jean-Henri Dunant. After witnessing the bloody Battle of Solferino with 40,000 casualties, Dunant wrote *A Memory of Solferino* in which he proposed the formation of an international relief organization. The Swiss-based organization chose for their symbol a red cross on a white background—the reverse of the color scheme of the Swiss flag. Clara was influenced by Dunant and began to consider forming a relief organization in the United States.

In 1873, Barton returned home. She spent the next four years convalescing from a nervous disorder that caused migraine headaches and periods of blindness. In March 1876, she moved to Dansville, New York, to improve her health at a sanatorium. After a year's rest with wholesome food in a peaceful environment, Barton completely regained her health.

While living in Dansville, Barton worked to bring the United States into the International Red Cross. She discovered that the reason for the resistance in the United States to joining the international organization was that it was considered a wartime relief organization. Barton pointed out the need for such an organization in addressing peacetime disasters, such as earthquakes and floods. She went to Washington, D.C., to convince President Garfield's cabinet of the importance of a U.S. role in the international relief organization.

When Barton returned to Dansville, the townspeople asked her to help form a local chapter of the Red Cross. On August 22, 1881, the first American chapter of the Red Cross was established in Dansville. The first disaster addressed by the chapter was a Michigan forest fire that took 500 lives and destroyed 1,500 homes. On March 16, 1882, Congress signed the Treaty of Geneva, which made the U. S. a member of the International Red Cross. Barton was appointed as the first president of the American Red Cross. She served in that position until May 1904. She died in Washington, D.C., on April 12, 1912.

* * *

Florence Nightingale and Clara Barton possessed many qualities in addition to empathy. Both were strong willed. Nightingale’s and Barton’s motivation to help others was stronger than their concern about risk, even risk to their own lives. Both had considerable ability to persuade others of the importance of their recommendations.

CHAPTER 3

OPTIMISM—ROLE MODELS

John Milton (1608-1674) Author of "Paradise Lost"

Helen Keller (1880-1968) Humanitarian and Author

"Optimism is the ability to see hope and stay positive in all situations and times, regardless of how bleak the present may be. When things are going well, it is quite easy to be upbeat and in good spirits. Success, however, demands that we be able to see hope and possibility even after major setbacks. One of the common denominators of successful people is their ability to bounce back after failures."

Harvey Deutschendorf, *The Other Kind of Smart*

JOHN MILTON—Author of "Paradise Lost"

"Yet I argue not
Against heaven's hand or will,
nor bate a jot
Of heart and hope; but still bear up
and steer
Right onward."

Milton, *Sonnet XXII*

John Milton was a highly regarded English dramatic poet. Milton wrote epics that are now appreciated principally by the academic community. His own life was also an epic. He had been imprisoned and had faced a possible death sentence for his support of the Lord Protector, Lord Cromwell, during the Reformation. Milton lost his sight at the age of 43; however, he wasn't deterred from writing a major work in his later years that he knew he was destined to write. Writing a magnum opus was his reason for being.

Milton's blindness has caused much speculation. Possible diagnoses include glaucoma, paralysis of the optic nerves, and detached retinas. Sight in his left eye was nearly gone by early 1650; he became totally blind during the winter of 1651-52 with his great work still unwritten. When his eyesight began to fail, his doctor advised him to spare his eyesight by writing less. He responded, "The choice lay before me between dereliction of a supreme duty and loss of eyesight . . . I could but obey the inward monitor that spoke to me from above . . . If my affliction is incurable, I prepare and compose myself accordingly." Milton said, "It is not so wretched to be blind as it is not to be capable of enduring blindness."

James II, when he was Duke of York, visited Milton and told him that his blindness was punishment from above for writing a justification of the execution of Charles I. Milton replied, "If Your Highness thinks that misfortunes are indexes of the wrath of heaven, what must you think of your father's tragical end? I have only lost my eyes—he lost his head."

Milton's attitude toward his affliction is summed up in the following autobiographical sonnet:

When I consider how my light is spent
Ere half my days in this dark world and wide,
And that one talent which is death to hide
Lodged with me useless, though my soul more bent
To serve wherewith my maker, and present
My true account, lest He returning chide;
"Doth God exact day-labor, light denied?"
I fondly ask. But patience, to prevent
That murmur, soon replies, "God doth not need
Either man's work or his own gifts. Who best
Bear His mild yoke, they serve Him best. His state
Is kingly: thousands at His bidding speed,
And post o'er land and ocean without rest;
They also serve who only stand and wait."

Milton's life was difficult; he was dependent upon amanuenses to whom he dictated. He relied heavily on his three daughters, who had been taught to pronounce six languages to read to their father. Unfortunately, they didn't understand what they were reading. The older daughters, Anne and Mary, considered the task drudgery, and, according to biographer Edward Phillips, were "condemned to a trial of patience almost beyond endurance." The youngest daughter, Deborah, was the only one who willingly helped her father.

Milton was in his 50s when he began his epic sonnet, *Paradise Lost*. Earlier, he had considered an English theme for this work, such as the legend of King Arthur and the Knights of the Round Table. In 1640, when he was in his early 30s, he had listed approximately 100 biblical and historical themes for plays that he documented in the *Cambridge Manuscript*.

Eventually, Milton rejected the subject of a narrative poem of heroes for that of a moral saga describing, on a grand scale, the battle between Good and Evil. He envisioned a battle fought by angels and demons for the benefit of humanity.

In the first part of *Paradise Lost*, Milton describes an unsuccessful rebellion in heaven, after which Satan, Beelzebub, Moloch, Mammon, and a host of lesser angels are expelled from heaven and sent to hell. The principal source for his work is the Bible, including the Apocrypha. Milton deals with the fall of man in the second part of the narrative. He discusses the temptation, in which Eve sins by the weakness of reason and Adam sins through the weakness of will, their expulsion from Paradise, and Christ's intercession for all mankind.

Milton's next work was *Paradise Regained*, which focuses on the temptation of Christ in the wilderness. He describes Christ's resistance to temptation in winning back for mankind that which was lost by Adam's sins. Satan is a much diminished figure in *Paradise Regained*, compared with his almost heroic proportions in the first two books of *Paradise Lost*. Critics don't consider *Paradise Regained* on the same level as *Paradise Lost*.

Milton's last work was *Samson Agonistes*, a story about the last years of Samson's life, done in the style of a Greek tragedy. Milton describes Samson's betrayal by the treacherous Delilah and how a human sinner is regenerated after reaching the depths of despair. Milton published *Samson Agonistes* in 1667, the same year that he published the less popular *Paradise Regained*.

When he was 21, Milton had set a goal to write a major epic for the ages, and he refused to let the loss of his sight keep him from his goal. He remained optimistic until, late in life, he accomplished his reason for being. Milton had a profound impact on later poets. The Miltonic form of the sonnet was used by Coleridge, Keats, and Wordsworth.

A. E. Housman gave Milton a rich tribute: "The dignity, the sanity, the unfaltering elevation of style, the just subordination of detail, the due adoption of means to ends, the high respect of the craftsman for his craft and for himself, which ennoble Virgil and the great Greeks, are all to be found in Milton and nowhere else are they in English literature to be found."

HELEN KELLER—Humanitarian and Author

"My life has been happy because I have wonderful friends and plenty of interesting work to do. I seldom think about my limitations, and they never make me sad. Perhaps there is just a touch of yearning at times, but it is vague, like a breeze among flowers. The wind passes, and the flowers are content. . . . I slip back at times. I fall, I stand still. I run against the edge of hidden obstacles. I lose my temper and find it again, and keep it better. I trudge on. I gain a little. I feel encouraged. I get more eager and climb higher and begin to see widening horizons."

Helen Keller, *The Story of My Life*

Helen Keller was a model of what the human spirit can do when challenged. She was above average in intelligence and in inquisitiveness. Her ability to overcome her triple handicaps of being blind, deaf, and mute is an inspiration to all of us. She could not have accomplished what she did without a very positive outlook and large measures of optimism.

Keller led a life of achievement, writing articles and books and supporting causes for the handicapped, particularly the blind. She received considerable recognition for her accomplishments. Her academic honors included honorary degrees from Harvard University and the University of Berlin as well as a Doctor of Laws degree from the University of Glasgow and a Doctor of Humane Letters degree from Temple University. She was invited to the White House by every President from Grover Cleveland to John F. Kennedy, and, in 1964, she was awarded the Presidential Medal of Freedom by President Lyndon Johnson.

Keller was a normal infant until the age of 19 months, when, due to an illness, she lost her sight, her hearing, and her ability to speak. Her resilience in overcoming her handicaps was exemplary. The accomplishments of her teacher, Anne Sullivan, were notable as well.

Keller's devastating illness occurred in February 1882. It was described by doctors as "acute congestion of the stomach and brain" and "brain fever," but it was probably scarlet fever. Helen's doctor did not expect her to live. Hope for Keller to overcome her disabilities came when her mother read Charles Dickens's

"American Notes," in which he described the progress made by a young girl who was blind and deaf and had been educated at the Perkins Institution in Boston.

At about the same time, Arthur Keller took his daughter to Baltimore for a comprehensive eye examination by the highly regarded oculist, Dr. Chisholm. He gave no encouragement for improvement but suggested to Arthur Keller that he consult with Dr. Alexander Graham Bell in Washington. Dr. Bell, the Scottish-American inventor of the telephone, had a life-long commitment to helping the deaf. He had been a teacher of speech for the deaf in Boston. Dr. Bell suggested that the Kellers contact the Perkins Institution.

The institution recommended Anne Sullivan as a teacher for Keller. When Sullivan arrived at the Kellers' home in Tuscumbia, Alabama, to take up her new responsibilities, she was pleased to find a healthy young girl who indicated early that she was clever. However, Sullivan found that Keller was an unruly, undisciplined child whose behavior was out of control.

Sullivan realized that she would have to establish her authority quickly if she hoped to succeed with her charge. Within several days, Keller demonstrated her unruliness by knocking out two of her teacher's front teeth. Keller would pinch Sullivan when she was disappointed and then lie on the floor and kick and scream.

Sullivan suggested that faster progress could be made if she and Keller were off by themselves. The Kellers realized the importance of establishing discipline and suggested that Sullivan and their daughter move to the garden house, which was a quarter mile from the homestead. After two weeks in the garden house, Keller realized that Sullivan was trying to help her. The young student became not only obedient but loving. Sullivan was overjoyed. Keller began to show a definite interest in learning.

On April 5, 1887, just over a month after Sullivan arrived in Tuscumbia, a significant emotional event occurred for Keller. Sullivan described it in a letter to a friend at Perkins, as cited by Keller in *The Story of My Life:*

> I must write you a line this morning because something very important has happened. Helen has taken the second great step in her education. She

> has learned that everything has a name, and that the manual alphabet is the key to everything she wants to know. . . . This morning, while she was washing, she wanted to know the word for "water" . . . I spelled "w-a-t-e-r" and thought no more about it until after breakfast. . . . We went out to the pump house, and I made Helen hold her hand under the spout while I pumped. I spelled "w-a-t-e-r" in Helen's free hand.
>
> The word coming so close upon the sensation of cold water rushing over her hand seemed to startle her. She dropped the mug and stood transfixed. A new light came into her face. She spelled "w-a-t-e-r" several times. Then she dropped on the ground and asked for its name. . . .

Keller was awakened to the possibilities now open to her; she learned at a frantic pace. During several hours in one day in April 1887, she added 30 words to her vocabulary. Her next goals were to learn to construct sentences and to learn how to read. In May 1887, Keller read her first story. Although Louis Braille had invented a system of printing books for the blind in which characters are represented by raised dots in 1829, no standardized technique for printing books for the blind was used at that time.

Sullivan suggested that Keller move to Boston to take advantage of the materials available at the Perkins Institution to teach the blind. Also, Helen would have the opportunity to meet other children who shared her handicaps. In May 1888, Keller began to learn Braille at Perkins. Keller set a goal for herself to learn to speak. Sullivan did not think that this was a good way for Keller to spend her energy; however, Keller insisted.

In March 1890, Keller enrolled at the Horace Mann School for the Deaf in Boston. She described the method used by her teacher: "She passed my hand lightly over her face, and let me feel the position of her tongue and lips when she made a sound. I was eager to initiate every motion and in an hour had learned six elements of speech: M, P, A, S, T, and I. I shall never forget the surprise and delight I felt when I uttered my first sentence: 'It is warm.'"

One had to speak slowly for Keller to understand what a person was saying. Her teacher also taught her how to lip read by placing her fingers not only on the lips of the person speaking but also on his or her throat.

Keller wanted to study at Radcliffe. Years later, President Woodrow Wilson asked her why she chose Radcliffe. She replied that she thought that they didn't want her at Radcliffe, and, because she was stubborn, she decided to go there. Keller carried a full course load. Sullivan went to all of her classes and spelled the contents of the lectures into Keller's hand. Keller was elected vice president of her freshman class.

While at Radcliffe, Keller enrolled in a composition course taught by a highly regarded Harvard professor. Her writing attracted the attention of the editors of the *Ladies' Home Journal*, who asked her to write her autobiography, which was published in 1902. *The Story of My Life* was a success as it had been when published in the *Ladies' Home Journal*. Keller's second book, *Optimism,* based on a 7,000-word essay that she wrote on the goodness of life while an undergraduate at Radcliffe, was published in 1903.

In 1906, Keller was appointed to the Massachusetts Commission for the Blind. She pioneered in bringing the problems of blind newborns to the attention of the public.

In 1909, Keller's third book, *The World I Live In,* was published. In 1927, her book, *My Religion*, was published, followed two years later by *Midstream: My Later Life*. Keller gave lectures sponsored by the American Foundation for the Blind and established the Helen Keller Endowment Fund.

In 1940, Keller wrote *Let Us Have Faith*, in which she discusses "the ultimate ability of man to conquer despair and tyranny." In 1955, her biography of Anne Sullivan Macy, *Teacher*, was published.

Keller died on June 1, 1968, of arteriosclerotic heart disease. She was an optimist for her entire lifetime. She said, "I believe that all through these dark and silent years, God has been using my life for a purpose I do not know. But one day I shall understand, and then I will be satisfied."

* * *

John Milton and Helen Keller were confronted with serious handicaps that they were sufficiently optimistic to overcome. Milton knew from an early age that he was going to write a magnum opus and did not let blindness prevent that accomplishment. Keller did not let being blind, deaf, and mute from the time of her infancy prevent her from having a lifetime of achievement. Milton and Keller are outstanding examples of resilience and determination, as well as optimism.

CHAPTER 4

PERSUASION / NEGOTIATION—ROLE MODELS

Heinrich Schliemann (1822-1890) Discoverer of Ancient Troy

Bill Gates (1955-) Founder of Microsoft Corporation

"People smart negotiators use their skills at tuning in and explaining things clearly to encourage acceptance and understanding. Empathy, tact, and humor can go a long way to foster partnership. And when we approach conflict resolution as partners, rather than adversaries, we can avoid wasting time bogging down in extraneous battles, saving our energy for the real issues at hand. The idea is to fix the problem, not the blame."

Mel Silberman, *People Smart*

HEINRICH SCHLIEMANN—Discoverer of Ancient Troy

"With his unshakable faith in Homer, his boundless energy and enthusiasm, his organizing ability, his resolute determination, and his unfailing persistence—all backed by abundant financial resources, which he had acquired by his own efforts—with all these qualifications, Schliemann overcame numerous obstacles and difficulties and achieved a brilliant success."

Carl W. Blegen, *Troy and the Trojans*

Heinrich Schliemann made his first fortune in the import-export business and his second fortune in the California gold fields. This allowed him to do what he really wanted to do with his life—discover ancient Troy.

Schliemann grew up in Germany but, as a young man, moved to Amsterdam. In 1844, he obtained a position with the largest import-export firm in the city. He invested successfully in imports from India and accumulated substantial savings.

As a boy, Schliemann had read about Troy and the memories had stayed with him. When he had sufficient wealth to finance his explorations, his thoughts returned to the stories of Homer and of adding to the world's knowledge. He wanted to walk the paths of Achilles, Hector, and King Priam and to uncover the ruins of Troy.

In 1858, Schliemann visited Greece for the first time and was captivated by it. He traveled around the world, ending up in Paris, where he attended the Sorbonne. Courses in archaeology rekindled his interest in Troy.

In 1868, Schliemann traveled to the Island of Ithaca, Greece, where he did his first excavation. According to legend, Odysseus, who ruled Ithaca, had joined Agamemnon and Menelaus in their campaign against Troy. Odysseus was shipwrecked returning from the expedition and did not arrive home for 10 years.

Odysseus's story, and the story of Penelope's patient wait for him, is told in the *Odyssey*. Schliemann's reading and his geographic instinct led him to the site of his first dig. Initially, Schliemann broke some artifacts in digging with a pick and did not keep accurate records of the depth and orientation of the objects. As he gained experience as an archaeologist, his discipline and methods improved markedly.

Schliemann and his workers uncovered a 10-foot by 15-foot stone room, 20 vases, clay female figures, and a few weapons. His findings were enough to reinforce his interest in archaeology. In traveling to a possible site of Troy in Turkey, he met Frank Calvert, an Englishman with experience in excavating ruins and in working with Turkish authorities. They investigated Bunarbashi, rumored to be the site of Troy, but neither man agreed with the rumors.

Schliemann and Calvert thought that a more likely site for Troy was the great mound at Hissarlik, which was closer to the sea than Bunarbashi. Calvert gave his new friend access to the part of the Hissarlik mound that he owned, but permission to dig on the other part would have to be obtained from the Turkish owners. Schliemann and Calvert had to apply for a firman (permit) before they could begin excavating. Schliemann surveyed the mound, which was 800 feet long.

Schliemann was told that his firman to proceed with excavation at Troy had been delayed. In April 1870, Schliemann hired laborers and began digging at Hissarlik without waiting for the firman. The team uncovered the ruins of a stone building measuring 40 feet by 60 feet, not large enough to be King Priam's palace. One of the few significant finds was a Roman coin with Emperor Commodus on one side and Hector, King Priam's son, on the other.

Two Turks arrived to complain that Schliemann was digging on their land. They would not accept a reasonable price for their property but Schliemann persuaded them to let the archaeologists dig.

To spur interest in the excavations, Schliemann wrote an article about his meager findings that was read by Turkish authorities, who prevented further digging. Schliemann met an official of the Turkish government. The enthusiastic archaeologist used his negotiating skills to ask the Turkish authority to convince the Turkish owners of the Hissarlik property to sell it at a fair price. The official persuaded the Turks to sell, not to Schliemann but to the Turkish government to ensure that any valuable artifacts belonged to the government.

Finally, in August 1871, Schliemann received the permit to dig at Hissarlik for which he had waited so long. The Turkish authority sent an "observer" to ensure that no valuable artifacts were carried away by Schliemann, who resolved not to turn over everything that he found to the Turkish official.

Excavation revealed foundations of undressed stone built on older foundations. They found dressed masonry, coins, and many small terra-cotta figures of owls, but nothing confirmed that it was the palace of King Priam. Schliemann did not think that the terra-cotta figures were from the time of Troy.

During the following summer, Schliemann's diggers found marble slabs inscribed with dedications, a bas-relief of Apollo and the four horses of the sun sculpted by a master, and nine large clay jars. These findings were meager, and the Turkish minister mistakenly accused him of hiding discoveries. Schliemann endured many hardships; living conditions were primitive, and he suffered from fevers.

In late May 1873, Schliemann found what he believed to be the outer wall of Priam's palace. When he found shiny material near the western gate, he dismissed the men so he could investigate further. The observer followed the diggers off the site.

Schliemann dug up a large copper container filled with gold, silver, and copper artifacts. He had made one of the greatest archaeological finds up until that time. It included bottles, cups, goblets, pots, vases, knifeblades, and spearheads as well as almost 9,000 gold rings and buttons. He also found gold diadems, headbands, ear pendants, and earrings that might have been worn by Helen of Troy. Schliemann immediately packed away the treasure.

When the observer returned to the site, he demanded to investigate all of the packing boxes. Schliemann sent him away. During the night, he conveyed his discoveries to Frank Calvert for forwarding to his home in Athens. In the morning, he allowed the observer to check all of the packing boxes and returned to Athens, where he documented his findings and buried them in multiple places for safety.

Schliemann published a detailed description of the treasure. The government of Turkey accused him of stealing their country's treasures. This grievance was the subject of many court cases. He was called a "treasure hunter" and a "gold seeker" until he told his accusers that he wanted to finance a museum to display the artifacts. He wanted to locate it in Greece, but he was not sure that the Greeks could resist the demands of the Turks.

England also wanted the museum, and Schliemann was received by Queen Victoria. The artifacts were put on display in

England, silencing those who had doubted the findings. Arthur Evans, a young archaeologist who later provided Schliemann with professional support, made a thorough study of the treasure.

Turkey settled the court cases for a payment of 50,000 francs and permitted Schliemann to return to Troy. The Turkish government provided no financing and agreed to a 50-50 split of any future findings.

Schliemann decided to excavate next at Mycenae in Greece. The Greek government gave permission to dig at Mycenae; however, like the government of Turkey at Hissarlik, they assigned an observer.

In 1876, Schliemann and 60 workmen began digging near the Lion Gate and found the usual goblets, vases, clay animals, and figurines. Schliemann also found a large rock tomb; he saw the gleam of gold under three bodies covered with clay. He crawled down a narrow passageway and found a silver cup, 14 gold laurel-leaf crosses, and 15 gold diadems.

Schliemann found another grave under which was a burial chamber containing three more bodies; he made a significant discovery of gold crowns and scepters, goblets, jewelry, plaques, vases, wine jars, and a thousand thin pieces of gold shaped into objects. The jewelry included gold necklaces, six double crosses, and eight diadems.

Schliemann moved to an area with darker soil and found a round stone altar with a hole for offerings to those buried beneath the altar. Under the altar, he found five bodies covered in gold with gold death masks over their faces. The discoveries included a gold crown, gold breastplates, and 11 large goblets, one of which he thought was the "cup of Nestor" described in the eleventh book of the *Iliad*. Also found were gold belts, brooches, large buttons, ornaments, pins, plates, 150 gold disks, and 400 gold coins.

Schliemann reported his success to the King of Greece, as quoted by Alan Honour in *The Unlikely Hero:*

> With extreme joy I announce to Your Majesty that I have discovered the tombs which tradition, echoed by Pausanias, had designated as the sepulchers of Agamemnon, Cassandra, Eurymedon and their companions who were killed by Clytemnestra

> and her lover Aegisthus. They were surrounded by a double circle of stone slabs which would not have been erected unless they were great personages. In the tombs I found immense treasures of the most ancient objects of pure gold.
>
> These treasures alone will fill a great museum, the most wonderful in the world, and for centuries to come thousands of foreigners will flock to Greece to see them. I work only for the pure love of science, and accordingly I have no claim on these treasures. I give them intact and with lively enthusiasm to Greece. God grant that these treasures may become the cornerstone of an immense national wealth.

Schliemann built a large home in Athens to house some of his collections. He retired there and wrote a book, *Trojan Antiquities,* a summary of his notes.

Schliemann began to experience pains in his ears, and his health was failing. He underwent an operation in Paris to ease his headache pain, but it was not successful. He returned home to Greece. On December 25, 1890, he collapsed on the sidewalk and was taken to the office of his doctor. He could not speak, and he was partially paralyzed. Schliemann died in his doctor's office.

Over time, the voices of Schliemann's detractors have been silenced. Sir Arthur Evans verified that Schliemann had, in fact, discovered King Priam's Troy. What Schliemann did not know was that he had also uncovered earlier civilizations that went back to 6000 BC. Schliemann's efforts were the foundation upon which later work was based.

In some circles, Schliemann is called the "father of modern archaeology." Schliemann's determination and ability to persuade helped him add to the world's knowledge and to our understanding of the origins of civilization.

BILL GATES—Founder of Microsoft Corporation

"Bill Gates's philosophy and success are inseparable from the Information Revolution. From the start, he wanted to create 'a tool for the Information Age that could magnify your brainpower instead of your muscle power.' He sees digital tools as the means of augmenting the unique powers of the human being: thinking, articulating thought, working together with other humans to act on thought."

Robert Heller, *Bill Gates*

Young Bill Gates was a very competitive child and a good student. He wasn't disciplined heavily, and his mother, Mary Gates, observed that, to a large extent, he did what he wanted to from the age of eight. By the time Gates was 11, he was ahead of his fellow students in the public schools and needed additional academic challenges.

Gates's parents enrolled him in the Lakeside School, an exclusive private prep school for boys in Seattle. Lakeside was known for its challenging academic atmosphere in which students were encouraged to develop their own interests.

In the spring of 1968, Lakeside provided access to a DEC PDP-10 minicomputer. Gates became a frequent user of the PDP-10. Paul Allen, Gates's future partner, who was two years ahead of him at Lakeside, was also hooked on the new technology. Gates's first programs were written in BASIC (Beginners' All-Purpose Symbolic Instruction Code). Gates, Allen, and two other students formed the Lakeside Programmers' Group to earn money using the computer.

In early 1971, the Lakeside Programmers' Group accepted a contract with Information Sciences, Inc., a Portland timesharing company, to write a payroll program. The four classmates formed a partnership, completed the project successfully, and were paid royalties. Allen graduated from Lakeside in 1971 and enrolled at Washington State University, where he majored in computer science.

During his senior year at Lakeside, Gates was offered a job with TRW Corporation in Oregon to troubleshoot application programs that ran on the PDP-10. Gates immediately called Allen, who had dropped out of Washington State, to work on the project. Gates returned to TRW for the summer before entering Harvard University. He became a more professional programmer while at TRW.

Gates spent many hours on the PDP-10 at the Aiken Computer Center at Harvard. His schedule was erratic; it included little time for sleep. He accepted a job programming for Honeywell in Boston that summer. He was joined by Allen, who stayed on at Honeywell after Gates returned to Harvard for his sophomore year. One of Gates's residence hall friends was Steve Ballmer, an applied mathematics major, who later played a significant role in the development of Microsoft Corporation.

In December 1974, Allen was walking across Harvard Square to visit Gates when he saw the January issue of *Popular Electronics* at a news kiosk. The cover had a picture of the Altair 8800 with the headline "World's First Microcomputer Kit to Rival Commercial Models." When Allen saw Gates, he told him, "Well, here's our opportunity to do something with BASIC."

The Altair 8800 was developed by Ed Roberts of Micro Instrumentation and Telemetry Systems (MITS) in Albuquerque, New Mexico. It was based on the Intel 8080 microprocessor chip. It had neither a keyboard nor a display. Since a high-level programming language hadn't yet been written for the Intel 8080 microchip, the Altair had to be programmed in machine language by flipping switches on the front panel. It responded by flashing red lights near the switches.

Programming languages available for mainframe and minicomputers at the time included FORTRAN (Formula Translation), which is a scientific language, and COBOL (Common Business-Oriented Language). No BASIC programming language had yet been developed for the Intel 8080 microprocessor. Gates called Roberts to tell him that he and Allen had developed BASIC for the Altair 8800 and would license MITS to sell their software for royalty payments.

After telling Roberts that they had a working BASIC, Gates and Allen worked furiously to develop it. They didn't have an Altair 8800 to use in developing the software so they developed their programs by simulating the Altair 8800 on the PDP-10 in the Aiken Computer Center. Allen observed, "We were in the right place at the right time. Because of our previous experience, Bill and I had the necessary tools to be able to take advantage of this new situation." In late February, Allen delivered the BASIC software to MITS in Albuquerque.

Allen moved to Albuquerque to get BASIC ready for the Altair 8800 and to make enhancements. In effect, he was the entire software development department for MITS; all of the MITS employees were working overtime to fill the high volume of orders for the Altair. The Altair was unreliable and had extremely limited functionality; nevertheless, customers willingly mailed $400 checks to MITS to buy them.

Gates worked in Albuquerque during the summer of his sophomore year at Harvard. Gates and Allen realized that they should establish a formal partnership. Microsoft was founded in the summer of 1975.

Gates and Allen signed an agreement giving MITS "exclusive, worldwide rights to use and license BASIC to third parties." The agreement included the key phrase: "The company (MITS) agrees to use its best efforts to license, promote, and commercialize the Program (BASIC)." Gates's father and an Albuquerque lawyer helped Gates draft the agreement, which pioneered software licensing agreements. Although he was only 19, Gates was the principal architect of the groundbreaking agreement.

Gates returned to Harvard in the fall and spent his time attending classes, studying, writing software, and negotiating agreements for Microsoft. Allen stayed in Albuquerque to work with MITS. In January 1977, Gates dropped out of Harvard. His parents weren't happy with his decision.

According to the agreement with MITS, Microsoft had to obtain permission from MITS to sell Intel 8080 BASIC to other companies. Roberts of MITS didn't block these sales unless they were to direct competitors, which initially wasn't a problem. However, as the personal computer industry grew, the agreement limited Microsoft's growth potential.

The Microsoft royalty agreement with MITS included a cap on royalties. Furthermore, Roberts was contemplating selling MITS. Gates realized that Microsoft had to get out of the agreement with MITS. He sent Roberts a letter terminating the agreement for several reasons, including Roberts's lack of success in using his "best efforts to license, promote, and commercialize BASIC." The agreement stipulated that any arguments would be addressed by an arbitrator.

On May 22, 1977, Roberts sold MITS. The new owner notified Gates that "it would no longer market BASIC or allow it to be licensed because it considered all other hardware companies competitors." This was counter to the "best efforts" provision of the agreement with Microsoft. The arbitrator sided with Microsoft in the hearing.

This decision played a significant role in the shaping of the software industry and of Microsoft's role in it. Both MITS and the new owner had underestimated their 21-year-old adversary, Bill Gates.

Gates and Allen realized that New Mexico wasn't the optimal location for a fast-growing software company. They considered two other locations, the San Francisco Bay area and Seattle. San Francisco was the location of Silicon Valley and many computer-related companies; however, Seattle was home. Allen had a strong preference for Seattle, and Gates felt that it would be easy to attract programmers to the Northwest. In December 1978, Microsoft moved to Seattle.

Software had three levels: the operating system; languages, e.g. BASIC, FORTRAN, and COBOL; and application software, such as word processing and spreadsheet applications. The operating system, usually written in a low-level language such as assembly language, performed tasks like selecting the portion of the disk to be written upon. Microsoft licensed the CP/M (Control Program for Microcomputers) operating system from Digital Research to use with their programming language packages.

In 1980, observing the success of Apple Computer and others in the personal computer market, IBM decided to enter the market. In July 1980, IBM contacted Gates to discuss Microsoft's possible participation in its personal computer development effort. IBM met with Gates, Allen, and Steve Ballmer, Gates's friend from Harvard, who had just joined Microsoft as assistant to the president.

In August, at a second meeting with IBM, Gates was asked if he could develop a BASIC program by April 1981. Gates said that Microsoft could do it. In September, IBM asked Microsoft to furnish FORTRAN and COBOL, in addition to BASIC.

In October 1980, Gates and Ballmer met with IBM in Boca Raton, Florida, to discuss a contract for developing software for the IBM personal computer. The Microsoft cause was aided by a conversation between Don Estridge, who was responsible for IBM's personal computer development, and John Opel, IBM's chief executive officer, several days earlier at lunch. Estridge mentioned to Opel that he was negotiating with Microsoft to develop software for IBM. Opel said, "Oh, that's run by Bill Gates, Mary Gates's son." Opel knew Mary Gates from serving on the national board of the United Way. The contract between IBM and Microsoft was signed on November 6, 1980.

For two years after the IBM personal computer was introduced, MS-DOS (Microsoft Disk Operating System) and CP/M vied for leadership of the operating system market for personal computers. Eventually, the success of IBM's personal computer ensured that MS-DOS would win the race.

On October 28, 1985, the board of directors of Microsoft Corporation met to decide whether to proceed with an initial public offering of Microsoft stock. On March 13, 1986, public trading of Microsoft's stock opened. Two and a half million shares were traded on the first day of trading, and Microsoft's stock was worth $661 million. Gates owned 45 percent of the total shares and Allen owned 28 percent. By March 1987, Gates had become a billionaire at the age of 31.

Microsoft was phenomenally successful throughout the 1980s. In February 1986, Microsoft moved into new facilities in Redmond, Washington. In 1987, Microsoft became the largest microcomputer software company in the world.

Bill Gates was the fundamental factor in Microsoft's success. He focused on addressing the problems and the future of Microsoft.

By 1996, Gates was worth over $14.8 billion and over five to six times that by the end of the decade. However, net worth is not the only measure of success; it certainly isn't Bill Gates's principal measure. He remained focused on the needs of the software industry and persevered in providing the software products to meet those needs.

As the twenty-first century approached, Gates began to withdraw from some Microsoft management activities, although he continued as Chairman of the Board. Gates and his wife, Melinda, founded the Bill and Melinda Gates Foundation, which has contributed billions of dollars to fight poverty and disease.

* * *

Schliemann and Gates were highly motivated individuals who were accomplished in persuading others to see their point of view—Schliemann in negotiating with Turkish and Greek authorities and Gates in negotiating early Microsoft contracts at a young age.

CHAPTER 5

LEADERSHIP—ROLE MODELS

Abraham Lincoln (1809-1865) A Leader for His Time

Franklin Delano Roosevelt (1882-1945) Led the U.S. Out of the Depression

"The superior leaders managed to balance a people-oriented personal style with a decisive command role. They did not hesitate to take charge, to be purposeful, assertive, and businesslike. But the greatest difference between average and superior leaders was their emotional style. The most effective leaders were more positive and outgoing, more emotionally expressive and dramatic, warmer and more sociable (including smiling more), friendlier and more democratic, more cooperative, more likeable and 'fun to be with,' more appreciative and trustful, and even gentler than those who were merely average."

Daniel Goleman, *Working with Emotional Intelligence*

ABRAHAM LINCOLN—A Leader for His Time

"To thousands who never saw him, but who know him through his letters and speeches, and through the record of his private and public life, he is an inspiration. The story of his overcoming the difficulties of his early life has put courage into many a young heart; his resolute stand by what he thought to be right has helped countless souls to be true to their duty; and the kindness and goodwill which flowed from his great heart—even to his foes—made the cherishing of malice and bitterness seem unworthy and shameful."

Wilbur F. Gordy, *Abraham Lincoln*

Abraham Lincoln had many strong qualities. Leadership was one; perseverance was another. He persisted in his ambition to attain public office while encountering three defeats along the way. In 1832, he was defeated in his first bid for public office when he ran for the Illinois State Legislature. However, he won in his second attempt for that office in 1834 and was reelected several times. In 1846, he was elected to the U.S. House of Representatives. He was defeated in his first bid for the U.S. Senate in 1855 and again in 1858 when he ran against Stephen Douglas.

In 1856, Lincoln began to develop a national reputation when he was considered as a candidate for Vice President at the Republican Convention; however, he didn't have enough votes to be placed on the ticket. In his campaign for the Senate against Stephen Douglas, Lincoln achieved celebrity status in a series of debates. During the Lincoln-Douglas debates, he gave his famous house-divided speech, as cited by Olivia Coolidge in *The Apprenticeship of Abraham Lincoln:*

> A house divided against itself cannot stand. I believe this government cannot endure permanently half slave and half free. I do not expect the union to be dissolved—I do not expect the house to fall—but I do expect it will cease to be divided. It will become all one thing or all the other. Either the opponents of slavery will resist the spread of it, and place it where the public mind can rest in the

> belief that it is on the course of ultimate extinction; or its advocates will push it forward until it shall become alike lawful in all States, old as well as new, North as well as South.

In February 1860, Lincoln gained additional national exposure from his speech at Cooper Union, New York City. His closing remarks were "Let us have faith that right makes might; and in that faith let us, to the end, dare to do our duty as we understand it." Newspaperman Horace Greeley stated that "I do not hesitate to pronounce it the very best political address to which I have ever listened, and I have heard some of Webster's grandest."

At the Republican Convention in Chicago in May 1860, Lincoln won the party's nomination for President on the third ballot, beating front-runner William H. Seward of New York. The real tests of Lincoln's leadership began immediately after he was elected. His cabinet included three of his rivals for the Presidency, and virtually every member of his cabinet considered himself superior to Lincoln and more capable of doing the President's job. Members of Lincoln's cabinet were:

William Seward—Secretary of State
Caleb Smith—Secretary of the Interior
Salmon Chase—Secretary of the Treasury
Gideon Welles—Secretary of the Navy
Simon Cameron—Secretary of War
Frank Blair—Postmaster General
Edward Bates—Attorney General

Secretary of State Seward actually suggested that Lincoln give him the powers of de facto President. President Lincoln responded that he had been elected President, that he would carry out the responsibilities of the office, and that no one could do it for him.

On April 12, 1861, just over a month after his inauguration, Lincoln was confronted with the beginning of the Civil War when the Confederates fired on Ft. Sumter in Charleston harbor. Many of the country's most capable generals were from the South. With its plantation economy and culture of chivalry, soldiering was considered a noble occupation. Lincoln had counted on the services of

Robert E. Lee as Commander in Chief of the Union army. However, after much soul-searching, Lee declared his loyalty to his native State, the Commonwealth of Virginia. Finding a general who was capable of leading the Union Army to victory in the field became a crucial test for the new President.

General Winfield Scott was the senior Union general, but he was in his mid-60s and wasn't considered a field commander. Lincoln's first appointment as Commander of the Army of the Potomac was General McDowell. McDowell was unequal to the task and his forces were dramatically defeated by Confederate General Beauregard at the First Battle of Bull Run.

The Army of the Potomac required further training, and General McClellan replaced General McDowell to provide it. General McClellan did an outstanding job with the training assignment, and he was a good administrator; however, he wasn't an aggressive general. In fact, he became extremely cautious on the eve of battle. McClellan was slow in attacking Richmond, and, within five miles of the city, he let the Confederates attack first. The Army of the Potomac was driven back in defeat.

The Army of the Potomac returned to Washington. By withholding support to General Pope, who commanded the Union Army facing Lee's forces, McClellan contributed to the Union defeat at the Second Battle of Bull Run. Lincoln replaced General McClellan with General Burnside, who was defeated with significant Union losses at Fredericksburg.

Burnside accepted the blame and was replaced by one of his severest critics, General "Fighting Joe" Hooker, who, in turn, was defeated with considerable loss of lives at Chancellorsville. Subsequently, General Hooker quarreled with General Halleck, Lincoln's military advisor, and resigned. He was replaced by General Meade, who pursued Lee's army north to Gettysburg to win one of the decisive battles of the war.

As Lee was retreating southward from Gettysburg, Lincoln was notified of General Grant's victory at Vicksburg and his capture of 32,000 men. Finally, the Union had found a general who could beat the Confederate army. After being promoted to Lieutenant General and placed in charge of all Union forces, Grant moved on Richmond. He sent a message to President Lincoln via Secretary of War Stanton, who had replaced Simon Cameron when Cameron was appointed Minister to Russia, "I propose to fight it out on this line if it takes all summer." Lincoln observed that "It is the dogged pertinacity of Grant that wins."

Lincoln displayed his leadership again in achieving the goal of freeing American slaves. He knew that timing was critical in freeing the slaves; however, he was criticized for his delay in taking action. He wrote the Emancipation Proclamation, but waited until McClellan's victory at Antietam to announce it.

In August 1861, General Fremont, Commander of the Western Department of the Union army, had announced that in his department, the slaves of owners who were fighting against the Union were free men. In May 1862, General Hunter had declared the freedom of slaves in Florida, Georgia, and South Carolina. In both cases, Lincoln rescinded the declarations. He received considerable criticism, but he persisted and announced the Emancipation Proclamation when he considered the time to be right.

The United States was fortunate to have had a President with Lincoln's personal qualities, including leadership, empathy, optimism, and emotional control, during his critical time in office. Historians consider him one of the five "great" Presidents of the United States. The consensus of historians is that he was the finest President in the history of the country.

In an interview, historian Doris Kearns Goodwin observed that Lincoln's Emotional Intelligence contributed heavily to his success. She noted that Lincoln was an excellent communicator, both in writing and in speaking, and that he relied heavily on teamwork. He had reason to question the loyalty of his cabinet members but he worked well with them and did not bear a grudge.

FRANKLIN DELANO ROOSEVELT—Led the U.S. Out of the Depression

"No matter whether Governor Smith wins or loses, Franklin D. Roosevelt stands out as the real hero of the Democratic Convention of 1924. Adversity has lifted him above the bickering, the religious bigotry, conflicting personal ambitions and petty sectional prejudices. It has made him the one leader commanding the respect and admiration from all sections of the land. . . . Roosevelt might be a pathetic, tragic figure but for the fine courage that flashes in his smile. It holds observers enchained."

New York Evening World

Franklin Delano Roosevelt, the only child of James Roosevelt II and Sara Delano Roosevelt, was born on January 30, 1882, at Hyde Park, New York. Roosevelt's mother had considerable self-confidence, a trait that she passed on to her son. He attended prep school at Groton and then enrolled at Harvard University.

After Roosevelt graduated from Harvard, he attended Columbia University Law School. Upon his graduation from law school, he joined a prestigious law firm specializing in admiralty law.

At the 1910 Democratic State Convention, Roosevelt was asked to run for the State Senate representing Duchess County, a perennial Republican stronghold. During the campaign, he said, "There is nothing I love so much as a good fight." He won, moved to Albany, and began to display his liberal, progressive philosophy.

In the 1912 presidential race, Roosevelt campaigned for his fellow progressive, Woodrow Wilson. When Wilson was elected President, he appointed Roosevelt Assistant Secretary of the Navy. Roosevelt served in the Department of the Navy until 1920.

Every summer, Roosevelt vacationed with his family on the island of Campobello in the Bay of Fundy. On August 10, 1921, he took his family for a sail and then overexerted himself helping to put out a forest fire. He swam in Lake Severn to cool off, jogged two miles back to the family's cottage, and later went for another swim in the Bay of Fundy, which was cold even in August.

Roosevelt had a temperature of 102 the next day, with pain and sluggishness in his left leg. His illness was eventually diagnosed as poliomyelitis. He never fully regained the use of his major leg muscles, but he never gave up trying to rehabilitate himself. Initially, he walked with crutches; later, he was fitted with leg braces.

In 1924, Roosevelt reentered politics by managing the New York State campaign for Al Smith as the Democratic Party's candidate for President. Smith asked Roosevelt to make the nominating speech for him at the Democratic National Convention in New York City. Roosevelt's speech, in which he referred to Smith as "the happy warrior of the political battlefield" was well received and placed Roosevelt's name before the public, even though Smith lost the election.

In 1928, Roosevelt again made the nominating speech for Smith at the Democratic National Convention. Democratic party leaders persuaded Roosevelt to run for Governor of New York. Smith lost the presidential election to Herbert Hoover, but Roosevelt won the race for the governorship.

Serving as Governor of New York, the nation's most populous State, was considered good training for the Presidency. Many of the staff Roosevelt eventually brought to Washington during his terms as President first served him in Albany, including many of his "brain trust" of advisors in his campaign for the Presidency in 1932.

On March 4, 1933, in the fourth year of the Depression, Franklin Delano Roosevelt was inaugurated as the 32nd President of the United States. In his inaugural address, he declared, as noted by James McGregor Burns in *Roosevelt: The Lion and the Fox:*

> This is preeminently the time to speak the truth, frankly and boldly. Nor need we shirk from facing honestly conditions in our country today. This great nation will endure as it has endured, will revive, and will prosper. So, first of all, let me assert my firm belief that the only thing we have to fear is fear itself—nameless, unreasoning, unjustified terror which paralyzes needed efforts to convert retreat into advance.

Roosevelt's first 100 days in office were hectic. He summoned a special session of Congress that lasted from March 9 until June 16. The first bill he signed was for the Banking Act that gave him control over the banks as well as all transactions in foreign exchange and the right to withdraw all of the gold in the country. Next, he submitted the Economy Bill to Congress to cut government salaries, enact an excess profit tax on dividends and profits, and reduce the federal government budget by 25 percent. A request to repeal Prohibition came next, and, on March 15, the stock exchange was reopened.

During the next two months, many of the New Deal agencies were created, including the Agricultural Adjustment Administration (A.A.A.), the Civilian Conservation Corps (C.C.C.) to provide jobs for unemployed youth, the Securities and Exchange Commission (S.E.C.) established by the Securities Act, and the Tennessee Valley Authority (T.V.A.). Other acts initiated at this time were the act that created the Home Owners Loan Association to provide mortgages, the Federal Relief Act, the Glass-Steagall Act that established the Federal Deposit Insurance Fund to guarantee savings deposits, and the Farm Relief Act. In addition, $3.3 billion was appropriated for public works.

On April 16, the United States went off the gold standard, causing many to question if Roosevelt had gone too far. The most sweeping legislation was the National Industrial Recovery Act, which established price controls, increased wages, provided for collective bargaining, abolished child labor, and prohibited unfair labor practices.

Roosevelt was the target of considerable abuse in the press. A "tax the wealth" slogan wasn't popular with the leaders of the financial community or captains of industry. However, the working man was for him. As his first term in office progressed, more legislation was passed. The Federal Emergency Relief Administration provided $50 million for direct relief, and the Civil Works Administration provided $1 billion to give four million men temporary jobs. In 1934, the Public Works Administration was established, followed in 1935, by the Works Progress Administration.

Many of these efforts were intended to prime the economic pump. Other acts instituted during Roosevelt's first term were the Fair Labor Standards Act, the Pure Food and Drug Act, and the Public Utility Act. Also created at this time were the Commodity Credit Corporation, the Export-Import Bank, and the Rural Electrification Administration.

The legislation that Roosevelt himself considered most important was the Social Security Act of 1935, which introduced unemployment insurance and old-age insurance to the country. In some respects, Roosevelt established a planned economy in the United States.

All of the organizations created by this legislation didn't work as planned. However, Roosevelt showed a willingness to take bold steps to lead the country out of the Depression and to persist in trying various alternatives until success was achieved. The same persistence he had shown in overcoming his paralysis due to poliomyelitis served him well. In addition to perseverance and leadership, his Emotional Intelligence skills included optimism, persuasive ability, and a talent for team building.

Roosevelt is considered by historians one of the five great Presidents of the United States. In fact, in recent years, he has been ranked by U.S. historians as the second-greatest President, behind only Lincoln.

* * *

Lincoln inherited a powder keg when he entered office and displayed outstanding leadership in leading the country out of the Civil War. FDR inherited an economic mess from President Hoover and led the United States out of the Great Depression with a willingness to try solutions until those that worked were found.

CHAPTER 6

EMOTIONAL CONTROL—ROLE MODELS

Mohandas Gandhi (1869-1948) Promoter of Passive Resistance

Martin Luther King, Jr. (1929-1968) U.S. Civil Rights Leader

"Managing your emotions means understanding them and then using that understanding to deal with situations productively. Because emotions are produced by an interaction of your thoughts, physiological changes, and behavioral actions in response to an external event, you can manage your emotions by taking charge of each component. . . . Then, because a distressful emotion is generally caused by a problem situation . . . we look next at how you can bring your emotional thermostat to a level that allows you to think productively. You can then use problem solving to come up with the best course of action to take to resolve the situation."

Hendrie Weisinger, *Emotional Intelligence at Work*

MOHANDAS GANDHI—Promoter of Passive Resistance

"When he died, Gandhi was what he had always been: a private citizen without wealth, property, title, official position, academic distinction, or scientific achievement. Yet the chiefs of all governments . . . and the heads of all religions paid homage . . . Men and women and children knew, or felt, that when Gandhi fell by the assassin's three bullets the conscience of mankind had been left without a spokesman. Humanity was impoverished because a poor man had died. No one who survived him had faced mighty adversaries at home and abroad with the weapons of kindness, honesty, humility, and nonviolence, and, with these alone, won so many victories."

Louis Fischer, *Gandhi, His Life and Message for the World*

Mohandas Gandhi accomplished more by the use of civil disobedience and passive resistance in achieving his goals than many generals of armies and heads of government achieved. Albert Einstein said, "In years to come men will scarce believe that such a one as this ever in flesh and blood walked on this earth." Gandhi observed, "Men say I am a saint losing myself in politics. The fact is I am a politician trying my hardest to be a saint."

Gandhi attended college in India and law school in London. In 1893, he moved to South Africa to undertake civil cases for a company controlled by a group of Muslim merchants.

In 1901, Gandhi returned to India, where he was greeted as a hero because of his social work in South Africa. He was asked to return to South Africa by the Natal National Congress because many of the reforms that he had implemented to protect the rights of Indians living in South Africa were eroding. Gandhi opened a law office in Johannesburg. He published a weekly newspaper, *Indian Opinion*, to provide a voice for the Indian community and to give advice on self-improvement. He believed "The good of the individual is contained in the good of all; that is, the more one gives to society, the more one gains personally."

Gandhi adhered to three principles in his life: to be celibate, to practice ahimsa—absence of violence, and satyagraha—truth-force or love-force. Ahimsa is more than non-violence; it is the respect for life and a positive reaching out to life in all of its forms.

Gandhi's definition of satyagraha was "the vindication of truth not by the infliction of suffering on the opponent but on one's self." One doesn't use violence on an adversary, but self-control is used since the opponent must be "weaned from error by patience and sympathy." His meaning is more than passive resistance, since satyagraha requires an ongoing interaction between adversaries in working out their differences.

In September 1906, the government of Transvaal passed the Asiatic Law Amendment Ordinance requiring all Indians to register, to carry a registration card at all times, and to submit to being fingerprinted. Gandhi addressed a meeting of 3,000 Indians in Johannesburg in which he described the "Black Act," and proposed that all Indians refuse to obey the law.

Gandhi and the other leaders were given a two-month jail sentence. He read Thoreau's *Civil Disobedience* during his stay in jail. He agreed with Thoreau's view that it is more moral to be right than to abide by an unjust law. In Thoreau's words: "The only obligation which I have the right to assume is to do at any time what I think is right." Gandhi and Thoreau knew that a minority, if sufficiently determined, can overrule the majority.

The restrictions imposed upon Indians by the South African government included restrictions on moving freely between provinces. In 1913, Gandhi planned another satyagraha civil disobedience. Gandhi went to New Castle to convince the mine workers, along with women and children—over 2,000 people in all—to march with him to Transvaal and, probably, prison. The government ignored his requests to repeal the unjust laws, so he marched with the crowd. He was arrested and given a nine-month jail sentence.

The British Parliament reacted when they heard that thousands of the government's subjects, including many children, had been sentenced to hard labor in the prison camps. A commission of inquiry was instituted about the time that Gandhi was released from prison. Gandhi planned a march to protest prison conditions, but a strike by the white South African railway workers began before he could start the march. This strike threatened to pull down the government, so he called off his march.

Prime Minister Botha and General Smuts appreciated Gandhi's decision and negotiated with him, even though Gandhi held no official office. On July 18, 1914, Gandhi returned to India. General

Smuts commented, "The saint has left our shores; I hope forever."

Smuts also wrote: "It was my fate to be the antagonist of a man for whom even then I had the highest respect . . . He never forgot the human background of the situation, never lost his temper or succumbed to hate, and preserved his gentle humor in the most trying situations. His manner and spirit, even then, as well as later, contrasted markedly with the ruthless and brutal forcefulness which is in vogue in our day." Gandhi's emotional control could not be described any better.

In January 1915, Gandhi arrived in Bombay. He found that living conditions hadn't improved in his absence, and that Hindus and Moslems were still antagonists. He worked to improve living conditions in India to prepare for independence from the British Empire. Gandhi was asked to arbitrate a demand for a pay increase for workers at a textile mill in Ahmedabad. He had friends on both sides of the conflict. The mill owners were heavy contributors to his commune; he knew them well. He suggested a compromise, which the owners rejected. The mill was temporarily shut down.

Many workers, who were now starving, were eager to accept the owners' terms. Gandhi urged them to hold out. One worker said to Gandhi that it was easy for him to hold out—he had plenty to eat. Gandhi wrote later, "The light came to me. Unbidden, the words came to my lips." He decided not to eat until the dispute was resolved, preferably by the owners' agreeing to his compromise. He would "fast until death" if required. The owners knew he was serious, and they didn't know how the workers would react if Gandhi died. After Gandhi had fasted for three days, they gave in, and the workers were given the compromise increase.

Incidents and atrocities in the Punjab brought Gandhi into politics in a way he hadn't planned. He became a leader of the Indian National Congress and the Indian Nationalist Movement. Previously, he had advocated dominion status for India, similar to the status of Canada and Australia in the British Commonwealth. Now he wanted the British out of India.

Gandhi participated in the drafting of a new constitution and opened up the membership of the Congress. He promoted the increased participation of the Moslem minority and stated a policy of noncooperation with the British. He organized a National Volunteer Corps, which consisted mainly of student activists, to help spread the concept of a satyagraha of noncooperation throughout India. One of his student volunteers was Jawaharlal Nehru, the son of Molital Nehru, president of the Indian Congress.

One goal was to become less dependent on imported British textiles. Initially, the British weren't worried by the noncooperation campaign, but as people burned their foreign-made clothes and picketed British clothing stores, it disrupted British control. Leaders of the National Congress and National Volunteers were arrested. By March 1920, 30,000 had been jailed, including Gandhi and the whole Nehru family. Gandhi was sentenced to six years in jail. He served just under two years, from March 1922 to February 1924, in solitary confinement.

With the leaders in jail, the Swaraj, or home rule movement, had languished and had become a struggle between the Hindu faction and the Moslem faction. When riots between Hindus and Moslems occurred in the Northwest Frontier Province, Gandhi began a fast scheduled for 21 days that would end with an improvement in Hindu-Moslem relations or with his death. Their relations improved during the fast, which became known as his "Great Fast," and groups composed of Hindus and Moslems visited him at his bedside. He fasted the entire 21 days; unfortunately, the improvement in Hindu-Moslem relations lasted only two years.

On January 1, 1930, Jawaharlal Nehru began his first term as president of the Indian Congress. Gandhi proposed protest activity against British rule. On March 2, 1930, he wrote to the Viceroy, noting that he held British rule to be a curse because "It has impoverished dumb millions by a system of progressive exploitation and by a ruinous, expensive military and civilian administration which the country could never afford. It has reduced us politically to serfdom. It has sapped the foundations of our culture. And it has degraded us spiritually." To demonstrate his displeasure, he announced that he would disregard the Salt Law.

The Salt Law established taxes on all salt consumed and prohibited the manufacture, sale, or consumption of salt not imported from England. The government was concerned by Gandhi's proposed action, but, once again, he had chosen a cause that was just. Salt is a necessary ingredient of the human diet for both peasants and the wealthy. However, the peasants were less able to pay the tax on a commodity that was available along India's shoreline.

On March 12, Gandhi and 78 of his followers began the 200-mile march from Sabarmati Commune to the coast. Twenty-four days later, 60-year-old Gandhi, wearing only a loincloth, waded into the Arabian Sea, reached down and picked up a small piece of salt from the beach, and ate it. By this act of eating one of God's gifts that the resident foreign government had forbidden him to eat, he had broken the law. It was precisely the type of gesture that the peasants could understand; furthermore, it caused injury to no one.

The Salt March gained attention not only all over India, but all over the world via press and radio. All of India began to break the Salt Law. Many were imprisoned, but there wasn't enough jail space for everyone. The government arrested Gandhi. Gandhi, Nehru, and many other leaders were jailed without a trial, and were held "at the pleasure of the government" under a little-used 1827 law. In late May, 2,500 National Volunteers advanced on the government-run Dharansa Saltworks. This unarmed mass faced 400 Indian police armed with lathis, steel-tipped bamboo clubs. A United Press staff writer reported:

> They marched steadily, with heads up, without the encouragement of music or cheering or any possibility that they might escape serious injury or death. The police rushed out and methodically and mechanically beat down the column. There was no fight, no struggle; the marchers simply walked forward until struck down.

The saltworks weren't damaged, but there was considerable damage to the world's view of British law enforcement.

Gandhi launched another civil disobedience campaign and was arrested on January 4, 1932; he was sent again to jail. By March, 35,000 Indians were in jail.

Britain's attention was diverted from India at the beginning of World War II in September 1939. When two neighbors of India were invaded by Japan, Britain knew that India had to be defended and reacted by taking away the few liberties that the Indians had.

Another passive resistance campaign commenced, causing jail sentences for Gandhi, Nehru, and 400 other Indian leaders. Twenty thousand resisters were in jail by 1941, but were released by the end of the year. Nehru and Gandhi offered to help the British, but only as a free nation. Britain offered dominion status at the end of the war.

In 1942, the leaders of Congress began a "Quit India" campaign and were jailed again. Gandhi left prison on May 6, 1944; he spent 2,338 days of his 77-year life in prison.

In February 1947, Lord Louis Mountbatten became the last Viceroy of India. His assignment was to withdraw from India. The Moslems threatened civil war if they weren't given the northeast and northwest territories. Congress had no alternative, and the two territories became Pakistan (the northeast territory became Bangladesh in 1971). This concession triggered widespread rioting.

Approximately 500,000 Indians were killed trying either to leave or to enter the new country of Pakistan; 15 million people were homeless. Gandhi began another fast until death. Moslems knew that they would be blamed for his death, so Moslem representatives joined with Hindu representatives at the bedside of the 77-year-old Mahatma. He ended his fast after four days.

On January 20, a bomb exploded near Gandhi while he was at prayer. It was thrown by a radical Hindu who disapproved of Gandhi calling Moslems his brothers and giving them two large sections of India. Gandhi told his friends, "If I die by the bullet of a madman, I must do so smiling. Should such a thing happen to me, you are not to shed one tear . . . if someone shot at me and I received his bullet in the bare chest without a sign and with Rama's [God's] name on my lips, only then should you say that I was a true Mahatma."

At about five o'clock the next evening, January 20, 1948, as Gandhi climbed the steps to his raised garden and walked toward an assembled crowd, Naturam Godse, a Hindu extremist, bent down to kiss Gandhi's feet. When he was pulled up, he fired three shots from a revolver into Gandhi's chest and stomach. Gandhi slumped to the ground, said "Hai Rama!" (Oh God) and died.

Gandhi left a great legacy to the world, including his saintliness and his nonviolent approach to the problems of life. His view of life was "I can wait 40, or 50, or 400 years—it is the same to me. Life goes on forever—we all persist in some form and inevitably victory is ours." It is difficult to think of a better example of emotional control than Mahatma Gandhi.

MARTIN LUTHER KING, JR.—U.S. Civil Rights Leader

"A final victory is an accumulation of many short-term encounters. To lightly dismiss a success because it does not usher in a complete order of justice is to fail to comprehend the process of achieving full victory."

Martin Luther King, Jr.

On February 25, 1948, Martin Luther King, Jr., was ordained a minister and became assistant pastor of Ebenezer Baptist Church in Atlanta, his father's church. After graduating from Morehouse College, King enrolled at Crozer Seminary. At Crozer he received straight As; he graduated first in his class. While at Crozer, King attended a lecture by the president of Howard University, who had just returned from a visit to India. He talked about the role of Mohandas Gandhi in freeing India from British rule by using non-violent means. He also discussed civil disobedience and passive resistance and made a profound impression on young King.

King was motivated to learn more about the Mahatma, and thought what he had heard "was so profound and fascinating that I left the meeting and bought a half dozen books on Gandhi's life and works." Later, he wrote in his book *Stride Toward Freedom*, "Not until I entered Crozer Theological Seminary . . . did I begin a serious intellectual quest for a method to eliminate social evil."

In 1951, King graduated from Crozer. He gave the valedictory address at commencement, won the Plafker Award as the most outstanding student, and received a fellowship to Boston University's School of Theology. In Boston, King met Coretta Scott, a voice student at the New England Conservatory of Music. They were married by Martin Luther King, Sr., on June 18, 1953.

King knew what he was going to do with his life. He explained his goal to his wife: "I'm going to be pastor of a church, a large Baptist church in the South. . . . I'm going to live in the South because that's where I'm needed."

In April 1954, the Dexter Avenue Baptist Church in Montgomery, Alabama, offered King the position of pastor. He and Coretta moved to Montgomery in August when she graduated from the conservatory. King continued to work on his doctoral dissertation and received his Ph.D. in Theology on June 5, 1955.

On December 1, 1955, an incident of national significance occurred in Montgomery. Rosa Parks, an African-American seamstress at a local department store, was riding home on a public bus after a busy work day. The bus driver asked her to give up her seat to a white passenger who had just boarded the bus. She was sitting in the first row of the African-American section of the bus, one row behind the white section; her feet hurt and she was carrying packages, so she refused to move. The driver asked her again to move. She responded again, firmly, "No."

The driver called the police; Parks was taken to the police station where she was booked for a violation of a city bus ordinance. She called E. D. Nixon, a member the National Association for the Advancement of Colored People (N.A.A.C.P.) to request bail. Nixon cheered when he heard that Rosa had been charged with violating the local bus segregation law. The N.A.A.C.P. was looking for a test case to challenge the blatantly unfair ordinance as far as the U.S. Supreme Court, if necessary. Nixon suggested a boycott of the city bus service using car pools. The boycott was virtually 100 percent successful on the first day.

Rosa Parks was found guilty and fined; the N.A.A.C.P. had their case. A new organization, the Montgomery Improvement Association (M.I.A.) was established to direct the boycott, and King was elected president. This surprised him, since he was new to the city and only 26 years old. He expected an older person to be nominated, but he willingly accepted the position.

Early in the boycott, King gave a rousing speech at a rally at the Holt Street Baptist Church. He said to the gathering, "If we protest courageously, and yet with dignity and Christian love, when the history books are written in the future, somebody will have to say, 'There lived a race of people, of black people, of people who had the moral courage to stand up for their rights. And thereby they injected a new meaning into the veins of history and civilization.'"

King received many life-threatening phone calls—as many as 30 to 40 calls a night. One evening he became depressed; he thought that he could no longer cope with his burden. He said later, "At that moment I experienced the presence of the Divine as I had never experienced Him before." He heard an inner voice that directed him to "Stand up for righteousness, stand up for truth, and God will be at your side forever."

On January 30, 1956, King spoke at an M.I.A. meeting at the First Baptist Church. Coretta was home with their daughter, Yolanda, when they heard something hit the front porch. They moved quickly from the front room to the back of the house as a bomb exploded; it destroyed part of the front porch and sent shards of glass all over the room they had just left.

King hurried home from the meeting. A crowd of African Americans, armed with clubs, knives, and guns, gathered in front of their home ready to retaliate for the bombing. He dispersed them by telling them to put away their weapons and to pursue a path of non-violence. He said, "I want you to love your enemies. Be good to them. This is what we must live by. We must meet hate with love." A better example of emotional control may not exist.

The city government tried to stop the boycott by enforcing a little-known law banning boycotts. Almost 100 M.I.A. members were charged, and King was the first one to be tried. He was found guilty; his sentence was a $500 fine or 386 days of hard labor. His attorney appealed the decision. The city passed an injunction to stop the use of car pools by declaring them to be a public nuisance. King was in court in November when he was told that the U.S. Supreme Court had ruled that Alabama's State and local bus segregation laws were unconstitutional.

King was gaining national attention. In February 1957, he became a national celebrity when his picture was on the cover of *Time* magazine and the cover article was about him. King was now viewed as the leader of 16 million African Americans.

In early 1957, a bill was sent to Congress to establish a civil rights commission to investigate violations of African-American rights, including their right to vote. The bill became the Civil Rights Act of 1957.

In early 1957, King and other African-American clergymen and leaders met to found the Southern Christian Leadership Conference (S.C.L.C.). King was elected president. He wrote the book that Harper and Brothers asked him to write, *Stride Toward Freedom*, a combination of an autobiography and a description of the Montgomery boycott.

Activity in the civil rights movement increased. On February 1, 1960, four African-American students from North Carolina Agricultural and Technical State University in Greensboro occupied stools at a segregated lunch counter at a Woolworth store. They weren't waited on, so they opened their books on the counter and began to study.

On the following day, six times their number engaged in a sit-in at the same Woolworth store. Within a week and a half, sit-ins occurred in South Carolina, Virginia, and other areas of North Carolina. By year-end, over 125 Southern towns had desegregated their lunch counters. The Student Non-violent Coordinating Committee (S.N.C.C.) grew out of the lunch-counter sit-ins.

Older adults continued what the students had started, and on October 19, 1960, King and 35 other African Americans were arrested in Rich's department store in Atlanta for trespassing when the waiters in the Magnolia Room refused to wait on them. Mayor William Hartsfield didn't like keeping King in the Fulton County jail; nevertheless, all except King were released promptly.

King had been arrested earlier in DeKalb County, Georgia, for driving with an expired license, fined, and placed on probation for a year. Fulton County officials complied with DeKalb County's request to turn King over to them. He was found guilty of violating his parole, denied bail, and sentenced to four months of hard labor at the State penitentiary at Reidsville, a prison for hardened criminals.

On October 25, Coretta received a call from Senator and presidential candidate John F. Kennedy, who offered his help in releasing her husband. Robert Kennedy, who managed his brother's presidential campaign, called the judge who sentenced King and expressed his thoughts about the injustice to King. He was released on bail within three days of JFK's call to Coretta.

On December 13, 1961, King spoke in Albany, Georgia, at a rally for an ongoing voter registration campaign sponsored by the S.N.C.C. Late the following day, he led a march to the City Hall. He and the other marchers were jailed for obstructing traffic, released within two days, and jailed again when they refused to pay a fine. Again, they were released after a short stay.

The S.C.L.C. chose Birmingham, Alabama, as the next target for a civil rights demonstration because of its history of segregation. The S.C.L.C. issued a demand to integrate public facilities and hire blacks for positions for which they hadn't been hired previously.

The Commissioner of Public Safety arrested and jailed 20 African Americans engaged in sit-ins in department stores. The following day, King led a group of 50 marchers on city hall. King was jailed again and subjected to abusive treatment.

Coretta called President Kennedy, and Kennedy talked to Birmingham officials about King's release. While in jail, King wrote his 6,400-word "Letter from Birmingham Jail." He wrote it in the margins of newspapers and on toilet paper and smuggled it out of jail. It was published as a pamphlet by the American Friends Service Committee and later was published in a magazine with a circulation of a million copies. After eight days, King was released on bail and recruited more marchers.

On May 2, over 1,000 marchers were greeted with high-pressure fire hoses that knocked them to the ground and into walls. Marchers were also confronted with snarling German shepherd police dogs that bit and scratched them. President Kennedy sent troops to Birmingham to assist in maintaining order.

On August 28, 1963, a high point of King's role as leader of the civil rights movement in the United States occurred on the mall between the Washington Monument and the Lincoln Memorial in Washington, D.C. A march on Washington was planned by African-American civil rights organizers to demonstrate the widespread support for the recently introduced civil rights legislation. Organizers anticipated a crowd of 100,000; however, the size of the crowd approached 250,000.

At 3:00 p.m., the last speaker of the rally was introduced, a man referred to as "the moral leader of the nation." King began to give his prepared speech, but the responsiveness of the crowd, which clapped in cadence with his speech, caused him to set aside the prepared text and speak extemporaneously from his heart—drawing on previous speeches he had given. The result was his famous "I have a dream" speech:

- I have a dream that one day on the red hills of Georgia the sons of former slaves and the sons of former slave owners will be able to sit down together at the table of brotherhood. . . .
-

- I have a dream that my four little children will one day live in a nation where they will not be judged by the color of their skin, but by the content of their character. . . .

- And when we allow freedom to ring, when we let it ring from every State and city, we will be able to speed up that day when all of God's children—black men and white men, Jews and Gentiles, Catholics and Protestants—will be able to join hands and to sing in the words of the old Negro spiritual, "Free at last, free at last, thank God almighty, we are free at last."

After the rally, President Kennedy invited the leaders of the march to the White House, where he promised his support in moving the civil rights legislation through Congress.

President Kennedy was assassinated on November 22, 1963. Fortunately, President Kennedy's successor, President Lyndon Johnson, was also a supporter of the civil rights movement, and the legislation was passed within a year. Enforcement of that legislation took much longer. *Time* magazine designated King "Man of the Year" for 1963.

On July 2, 1964, President Johnson signed the Civil Rights Act, authorizing the integration of public facilities and public schools. Civil rights leaders were invited to the White House for the signing ceremony in the East Room.

In October 1964, the Norwegian Parliament selected King for the Nobel Peace Prize. At 35, he was the youngest recipient of one of the most prestigious honors in the world, awarded for contributions to international peace.

The civil rights leaders were pleased with the passage of the Civil Rights Act and pushed for a Voting Rights Act. In some areas of the deep South, blacks were terrorized at polling places.

The S.C.L.C. chose Selma, Alabama, where only 383 of 15,000 African Americans were registered to vote, as the site for voting rights activity. The sheriff arrested 226 African Americans merely for attempting to register to vote. On March 7, 1965, the S.C.L.C. marched from Brown Chapel to the Edmund Pettus bridge over the Alabama River, where they were attacked by the sheriff's troopers. Almost 80 of the 600 marchers were treated for broken ribs and collar bones, fractured skulls, head cuts, and many other injuries on what was called "Bloody Sunday."

These incidents motivated President Johnson to plead for voting rights. He stated that "This time, on this issue, there must be no delay, no hesitation, and no compromise with our purpose." African Americans were entitled to "the full blessing of American life," and "their cause must be our cause, too." Everyone must strive to "overcome the crippling legacy of bigotry and injustice. And . . . we shall . . . overcome." On August 6, 1965, the Voting Rights Act was signed into law by President Johnson.

King and his followers next turned their attention to the economic inequality faced by African Americans. Initially, their efforts were concentrated in Chicago. However, when the striking garbage collectors of Memphis requested King's help, he went to Tennessee for a rally on April 3, 1968.

On April 4, King was joined at the Lorraine Motel by his brother, A. D., and several friends. Just after 6:00 p.m., King stood on the balcony outside room 306 with Hosea Williams, Jesse Jackson, and Ralph Abernathy. As they prepared to leave to go to dinner, King was shot in the neck and lower right side of his face by a single bullet fired by James Earl Ray from a rooming house across the street.

King died at about 7:00 p.m. in a Memphis hospital. His body was returned to Atlanta for his funeral at the Ebenezer Baptist Church on April 9, 1968. Over 60,000 people attended the funeral service, 800 inside the church and the rest outside, who listened to the service on loudspeakers. He was buried in South View Cemetery in Atlanta, where his paternal grandfather was buried. The epitaph on his crypt is "Free at last, free at last. Thank God Almighty, I'm free at last." During the course of his struggle, he said, "If you are cut down in a movement that is designed to save the soul of a nation, then no other death could be as redemptive."

* * *

Gandhi and King displayed exemplary emotional control in obtaining results with passive resistance. They knew that they could accomplish their goals by nonviolent means.

CHAPTER 7

SOCIAL RESPONSIBILITY—ROLE MODELS

Dorothy Day (1897-1980) Care Giver to the Poor and the Outcast

Mother Teresa (1910-1997) Comforter of the Destitute

"The saying of the seventeenth century English author John Donne: 'No man is an island'. . . encompasses the essence of the concept of social responsibility. We are all on earth together and our actions, or lack of them, impact a lot of people around us. We are socially responsible to the degree that we see ourselves as being part of something larger than ourselves. Socially responsible people have a sense of duty to make the world a better place in which to live."

Harvey Deutschendorf, *The Other Kind of Smart*

DOROTHY DAY—Care Giver to the Poor and the Outcast

"We were richly blessed to have her among us. . . . She was an ordinary woman whose faith caused her to do extraordinary things. The Gospel caught fire in this woman and caused an explosion of love. Perhaps the most important thing we can say is that she taught us what it means to be a Christian. She was a follower of Jesus Christ who fell in love with His kingdom and made it come alive in the most wretched circumstances of men and women. . . . Dorothy's heart never failed us."

Sojourners Magazine

Dorothy Day was born in New York City to a middle-class family. When she was in her teens, her father was a journalist in Chicago, where the family lived on the South Side. Day left the University of Illinois at Urbana after two years to work in New York City for *The Call,* a Socialist newspaper. She became a part of the radical Greenwich Village scene.

Day was not as interested in ideology as she was in observing the people and the conditions around her. She was an idealist with a strong sense of justice. She maintained these interests for the rest of her life. She wrote pamphlets observing the poverty and human suffering in the post-World War I era. She was an avid reader who enjoyed the New York intellectual scene. She knew some of the writers, including Hart Crane, Max Eastman, John Dos Passos, Eugene O'Neill, and Malcolm Cowley.

Day was first jailed in 1917 in Washington, D.C., where she had gone to march in a suffragist parade. Upon her return to New York, she left *The Call* and went to work for *The Liberator,* a radical magazine.

Day moved to Chicago, where she was jailed for the second time, along with her fellow activists of the International Workers of the World, known as "Wobblies." She was impressed with the kindness of the prostitutes in jail with her. They displayed a stubborn determination and generosity towards her.

At age 28, Day returned to New York and rented a cottage on the beach in Staten Island. She entered into a common law marriage and had a daughter. Her common law husband did not want a child. Also, about that time, she began to have doubts about her past life.

Baptized an Episcopalian, she began to consider converting to Catholicism. This was the final straw for her common law husband. He left her.

In her autobiography, *The Long Loneliness,* Day noted, "Something happened to me when I was around 25. I think I began to see myself drifting toward nowhere. I had lived a full and active life, and I was glad I had met so many good people, interesting and intelligent people. But I yearned for something more than a life of parties and intense political discussions."

Day's daughter was baptized in July 1927, and Day was baptized shortly afterwards. She observed, "I think I realized on the day I was baptized how long I had been waiting for that moment—all my life." She felt that her life was just beginning. In his biography of Dorothy Day, Robert Coles observes, "She had married into the church, not as a nun does, for she was hardly eligible for that vocation, but as her own kind of lay convert, and she was ready to give herself, voluntarily, body and mind and soul to an institution, no matter the doubts weighing on her."

During the Great Depression, Day was upset by the widespread poverty and the men and women walking the streets. She was concerned that neither the Church nor any of the institutions of the country were willing to help with food, shelter, and clothing. She wrote articles for *Commonweal,* a liberal Catholic magazine. She traveled to Washington, D.C., to observe a "hunger march." Upon her return to New York, she found a man named Peter Maurin waiting for her.

Maurin had grown up in France, where he was a member of a Catholic brotherhood who taught the poor. He wrote "Easy Essays" stating the nature of social problems with suggestions for practical responses to them in the spirit of the teachings in the Bible. Day and Maurin recognized the similarity of their views and their willingness to combine politics and religion as activists. Maurin became Day's mentor.

In 1933, Day and Maurin began to publish *The Catholic Worker* with very limited funds. Within a few years, it had a circulation of over 150,000. Shortly after they began to publish *The Catholic Worker,* Maurin said, "We need houses of hospitality to give the rich an opportunity to serve the poor." As Robert Cole observed in his biography of Day, "Maurin envisioned . . . a place where 'works of mercy' were offered and acknowledged in a person-to person fashion, as opposed to the faceless, bureaucratic procedures of the welfare state. . . . "

Day and Maurin began their first hospitality house with little money, not much of which came from the rich. The difference between their houses of hospitality and those of other organizations was that Day and Maurin lived there. Maurin didn't even have a room. He would return from a trip and have no place to sleep. The first house of hospitality was a rented apartment, "a rat-ridden place, heatless and filthy, abandoned even by slum dwellers."

As Cole describes, "They started . . . preparing soup, serving food to the homeless, finding clothes for them, offering them, when possible, a place to sleep, and very important, sitting with them, trying to converse, hoping in some way to offer them friendship and affection." Eventually, they had over 30 houses of hospitality.

Not all of the young adult volunteers were Catholics; in fact, some were atheists and agnostics. Cole also notes: "The hospitality houses are places where one can do concrete work on behalf of others. Many young men and women who feel within themselves surges of idealism don't know what to do about it. A skeptic might say they don't look hard enough, but it isn't always easy for people to find opportunities for charity in the biblical sense of the word, free of the implication of condescension. In hospitality houses, there is an immediacy to the charitable gesture, a directness, unmediated by bureaucracy and self-consciousness, that many young people find appealing."

Day died on November 29, 1980, three weeks after her 83rd birthday. She was active in publishing *The Catholic Worker* and in working in the houses of hospitality until her death.

Dorothy Day is an outstanding example of an individual who started out in life on a path that she realized would not lead to a life of accomplishment. She changed her lifestyle and spent the rest of her life helping the poor and the disadvantaged. She is a prime example of social responsibility.

MOTHER TERESA—Comforter of the Destitute

"Someone will ask, 'What can I do to help?' Her response is always the same, a response that reveals the clarity of her vision. . . . 'Just begin, one, one, one,' she urges. 'Begin at home by saying something good to your child, to your husband or your wife. Begin by helping someone in need in your community, at work, or at school. Begin by making whatever you do something for God.'"

Mother Teresa, "Words to Love By"

Young Agnes Gonxha realized that the religious life was to be her vocation when she was 12. The idea to become a missionary occurred to her when she was 14. At the age of 18, she joined the Loreto Order of nuns who worked in India. On May 24, 1931, Agnes took her first vows of poverty, chastity, and obedience as a nun. She chose the name Teresa after Saint Thèrése of Lisieux, the little flower of Jesus, a Carmelite nun who believed that the most menial tasks were forms of worship if they were done to help others or to serve God. Sister Teresa's first assignment was at the Loreto convent school in Darjeeling, where she also helped at the hospital. There she was introduced to poverty and suffering; conditions were worse than she had expected.

Upon completion of her assignment in Darjeeling, Sister Teresa taught Indian and Anglo-Indian girls from wealthy families at St. Mary's, the Loreto convent school in the Entally district of Calcutta. On May 14, 1937, she took her final vows as a Sister of Loreto. She became principal of St. Mary's School.

Sister Teresa was happy as a teacher with the Sisters of Loreto in Calcutta. However, she felt challenged to do more to help the people of the slums. She knew that to reach the poor she would have to work outside of the convent. Earlier, she had received a call to be a nun; on September 10, 1946, she received "the call within a call," as cited by Eileen Egan in *Such a Vision of the Street:*

> And when that happens the only thing to do is to say "Yes." The message was quite clear—I was to give up all and follow Jesus into the slums—to serve Him in the poorest of the poor. I knew it was

> His will that I had to follow Him. There was no doubt that it was to be His work. I was to leave the convent and work with the poor, living among them. It was an order. I knew where I belonged, but I did not know how to get there.

From her bedroom window, Sister Teresa could see the slums of Motijhil. She wanted to go there to help the needy, but nuns were only allowed out of the convent for emergencies, such as going to the hospital. Sister Teresa also saw the poverty first-hand when going back and forth through the slums to teach at St. Teresa's School, another Loreto convent school. She enjoyed her work at the convent schools for almost 20 years as a novice and as a nun, but she wanted to do something to help the poor and those dying from starvation and disease.

When Sister Teresa received "the call within a call," she knew that she had to go into the slums to help the poorest of the poor. The Archbishop was reluctant to allow her to establish a new congregation in the slums. In August 1947, however, permission was granted. Sister Teresa was 38 years old when she began her work there. She had no detailed plan; in her opinion, leaving the Loreto convent was a great sacrifice, probably the most difficult thing that she ever did. Initially, she lived with the Little Sisters of the Poor, whose mission was to help destitute elderly people.

Sister Teresa started a school in Motijhil, the slum adjacent to the Loreto convent. She had no money for school equipment and supplies, so she began by scratching letters in the dirt with a stick. Her five students the first day grew to 40 very quickly. It was lonely work, however, and her problems seemed insurmountable. She realized that to understand the poor, she had to live among them. In March 1949, one of her students at Loreto joined her in her mission. Within a year, 10 young sisters had volunteered to help her in her work.

In 1950, Mother Teresa formed the Missionaries of Charity with the Pope's blessing. By the late twentieth century, 300 houses of Missionaries of Charity were located in over 70 countries. During a time when vocations dwindled in the Church, the Missionaries of Charity expanded to over 4,000 sisters and brothers.

The Archbishop of Calcutta applied to the Office of the Propagation of the Faith in Rome for independent status for Sister Teresa's organization. She prepared a constitution that added a fourth vow of "wholehearted free service to the poorest of the poor" to the vows of poverty, chastity, and obedience. On October 7, 1950, she became Mother Superior of the Missionaries of Charity.

Mother Teresa drafted a decree for the new order: "To fulfill our mission of compassion and love to the poorest of the poor we go:

- seeking out in towns and villages all over the world even amid squalid surroundings the poorest, the abandoned, the sick, the infirm, the leprosy patients, the dying, the desperate, the lost, the outcasts
- taking care of them
- rendering help to them
- visiting them assiduously
- living Christ's love for them
- awakening their response to His great love"

In *A Gift for God*, Mother Teresa offered advice to novices in caring for the poor and the sick: "Speak tenderly to them. Let there be kindness in your face, in your eyes, in your smile, in the warmth of your greeting. Always have a cheerful smile. Don't only give your care, but give your heart as well." In her opinion, "The poor deserve not only service and dedication but also the joy that belongs to human love." In each of the "poorest of the poor" to whom she ministered, she "saw her God Himself, in distressing disguise." She said, "It is Christ you tend in the poor. It is His wounds you bathe, His sores you clean, His limbs you bandage."

Mother Teresa asked Calcutta's public health organization for their support in caring for terminally ill patients. It found an abandoned building that she could use. The Missionaries of Charity established the Place of the Immaculate Heart in the building.

The Place of the Immaculate Heart accepted the destitute and dying of all faiths, including Christians, Hindus, and Muslims. All were provided the opportunity to die with dignity. No attempt was made to convert members of other faiths to Catholicism.

Mother Teresa's objective in establishing the Home for the Dying was to provide "beautiful deaths." She said, "A beautiful death is for people who lived like animals, to die like angels—loved and wanted." The Home for the Dying housed men and women with many diseases, including cancer, dysentery, malaria, malnutrition, leprosy, and tuberculosis.

Mother Teresa paid particular attention to sufferers of Hansen's disease, or leprosy. She knew that administering sulfone drugs and providing a balanced diet brought improvement in virtually all cases of leprosy. In fact, the disease was curable if caught early enough. Mother Teresa opened rehabilitation centers for lepers. She was also instrumental in founding the Town of Peace for them, 200 miles from Calcutta.

When poor women with children died at the Home for the Dying, the Missionaries of Charity cared for the orphans. By 1955, so many children needed housing and food that Mother Teresa rented a building near the Order's headquarters and founded the Children's Home of the Immaculate Heart. Young teenage girls were brought in off the street to help take care of the children. Mother Teresa provided a small dowry for these girls when they were of marriageable age. Without a dowry, a girl would never find a husband and have the security of marriage.

In 1960, Mother Teresa made one of her first trips outside of India. She was invited by the National Council of Catholic Women to speak at its convention in the U.S. She also spoke with a representative of the World Health Organization at the United Nations about conditions facing lepers in India. In New York, she met Dorothy Day, co-founder of the Catholic Workers Movement, which published the *Catholic Worker.* Mother Teresa and Day remained friends until Day's death in 1980.

Mother Teresa expanded the Missionaries of Charity outside of Calcutta in the early 1960s, including a home for the dying in Delhi. Houses to aid the poor and the dying were established in two districts, and a leprosy clinic was established in a third. By 1962, nuns had been sent to 30 centers outside of Calcutta.

In March 1963, Mother Teresa added a group of young men to perform charitable services similar to those provided by the nuns. Twelve young men became the first members of the Missionary Brothers of Charity. Brothers could work in areas that were difficult for nuns, such as Phnom Penh, Cambodia, and Viet Nam. They fed and sheltered boys from the streets and were responsible for the men's ward at the Home for the Dying. They worked with the sick and the terminally ill, drug addicts, juvenile delinquents, lepers, and mental patients. Within a short time, they had hundreds of volunteers and had established 44 houses around the world.

In 1965, Mother Teresa opened her first mission outside of India, in Venezuela. Two years later, a mission was established in Ceylon (Sri Lanka). In the middle of her career, Mother Teresa summarized her outlook on her calling, as cited by Charlotte Gray in *Mother Teresa:*

> In these 20 years of work amongst the people, I have come more and more to realize that it is being unwanted that is the worst disease that any human being can ever experience. Nowadays we have found medicine for leprosy and lepers can be cured. . . . For all kinds of diseases there are medicines and cures. But for being unwanted, except when there are willing hands to serve and there's a loving heart to love, I don't think this terrible disease can ever be cured.

If we were to look for an example of social responsibility, of a person motivated to serve God by helping others, we would need to look no further than Mother Teresa. What can one person do to address the world's ills? Mother Teresa showed us.

* * *

Dorothy Day and Mother Teresa are excellent examples of individuals who gave their lives to helping others. They not only helped the poor and needy, they lived with them in their neighborhoods. Day is an outstanding role model of a person who lived a fast life while young but who realized that she should be doing more. She turned her life around and dedicated herself to serving others.

CHAPTER 8

MOTIVATION—ROLE MODELS

Frederick Douglass (1818-1895) Civil Rights Leader and Editor

Elizabeth Blackwell (1821-1910) First U.S. Woman Doctor

"Motivation is the word used to describe those processes that can (a) arouse and instigate behavior, (b) give direction or purpose to behavior, (c) continue to allow behavior to exist, and (d) lead to choosing or preferring a particular behavior. A motive is any condition within a person that affects his or her readiness to initiate or continue any activity or sequence of activities."

Raymond J. Wlodkowski, *Motivation in Education*

FREDERICK DOUGLASS—Civil Rights Leader and Editor

"It rekindled the few expiring embers of freedom and revived within me a sense of my own manhood. It recalled the departed self-confidence, and inspired me again with a determination to be free. He can only understand the deep satisfaction which I experienced, who has himself repelled by force the bloody arm of slavery. I felt as I never felt before. It was a glorious resurrection, from the tomb of slavery to the heaven of freedom. My long-crushed spirit rose, cowardice departed, bold defiance took its place, and I now resolved that, however long I might remain a slave in form, the day had passed forever when I could be a slave in fact."

Frederick Douglass, upon winning a fight with a "slave breaker"

Douglas T. Miller, *Frederick Douglass and the Fight for Freedom*

Frederick Douglass was born in February 1818 in Talbot County on the eastern shore of Maryland. His mother, Harriet Bailey, was a slave and his father, whom he never met, was a white man. His master was Captain Aaron Anthony.

In March 1826, Frederick was sent to live with a member of Anthony's family, Hugh Auld, in Baltimore. Living in Baltimore was a good experience for him; he had many opportunities to learn.

Thomas Auld, Frederick's legal owner, brought him back to rural slavery in 1833. He was not completely obedient, so Auld hired him out to an overseer who had reputation as a "slave breaker." After he had endured six months of flogging and other mistreatment, he turned on the slave breaker in a two-hour fight that he won. After that, the overseer didn't bother him, but he was even more committed to winning his freedom. Thomas Auld sent him back to Hugh Auld in Baltimore. He became an experienced caulker in a boatyard, where competition for jobs was fierce between poor white immigrants and slaves. He was attacked and badly beaten because he was thought to have taken a job from a white immigrant.

Frederick continued his self-education by joining the East Baltimore Mental Improvement Society, a debating club. An argument with Hugh Auld motivated Frederick to board a northbound train and escape. Despite some tense moments when he saw two local men who could identify him as a slave, he arrived in Philadelphia safely and then continued on to New York City.

Frederick stayed with David Ruggles, publisher of the antislavery quarterly, *The Mirror of Slavery*. Ruggles, who was active in the underground railroad, suggested that he move farther north. Frederick traveled to New Bedford, Massachusetts, where he hoped to find work as a caulker, and lived with Nathan Johnson and his wife. Johnson suggested that because Frederick was an escaped slave, he should change his name. Johnson had just finished reading Sir Walter Scott's *Lady of the Lake*; he suggested the surname of "Douglass," the name of the Scottish lord and hero. Frederick Bailey became Frederick Douglass.

When Douglass looked for work as a caulker, he found that prejudice existed in the North as well as the South. White caulkers did not want to work with African Americans. He was forced to take odd jobs as a common laborer. One day he found a copy of William Lloyd Garrison's antislavery newspaper, *The Liberator,* and it changed his life.

Garrison was a strong-willed abolitionist. In addition to being an editor, Garrison had helped to establish the New England Anti-Slavery Society. Douglass subscribed to Garrison's paper and was moved by it.

Douglass attended the annual meeting of the New England Anti-Slavery Society in New Bedford on August 9, 1841, and a meeting the next day on the Island of Nantucket. At the second meeting, Douglass was asked to speak. Although he was nervous, he spoke movingly about his life as a slave and was well-received.

Douglass was asked to become a full-time lecturer for the organization. He reluctantly accepted a three-month assignment and stayed for four years. He improved his oratorical skills and became one of the Society's most popular lecturers. On September 15, 1843, he was severely beaten in Pendleton, Indiana. He escaped with a broken wrist and bruises. Abolitionist newspaper editor Elijah Lovejoy was killed in Alton, Illinois, while defending his press from an incensed mob. William Lloyd Garrison was dragged through the streets of Boston with a rope around his waist and almost lost his life.

During the winter and early spring of 1844-45, Douglass left the lecture circuit to write an autobiography, *The Narrative of the*

Life of Frederick Douglass, an American Slave. In August 1845, he went on a successful lecture tour of England, Ireland, and Scotland.

One month after Douglass's return to America, two English women raised money and negotiated for his freedom. They contacted American agents to buy his freedom from the Aulds for $711.66. The deed of manumission was filed at the Baltimore Chattel Records Office on December 13, 1846, and Douglass was a free man.

Douglass returned to England for a lecture tour in 1847. Upon his return to America, he proceeded with plans to publish an anti-slavery newspaper. His British friends raised money to help him get started. He was surprised when Garrison advised against it. Garrison did not want competition for his own newspaper.

Douglass started his newspaper despite Garrison's counsel against it. He knew that he would have to choose a base far from Garrison's in New England. Douglass chose Rochester, New York, a booming city of 30,000 on the Erie Canal, where he had been well-received on the lecture circuit in 1842 and 1847. Douglass moved his family there on November 1, 1847.

In December 1847, the first edition of his newspaper, *North Star*, was published. He named it *North Star* because the North Star was the guide that the slaves used when escaping from the South to freedom.

Douglass supported the Woman's Rights Movement. On July 14, 1848, his *North Star* carried the announcement: "A convention to discuss the Social, Civil, and Religious Condition and Rights of Women will be held in the Wesleyan Chapel at Seneca Falls, New York, the 19th and 20th of July instant." The masthead that Douglass used for the *North Star* was: "RIGHT IS OF NO SEX—TRUTH IS OF NO COLOR."

In 1851, the *North Star* merged with the *Liberty Party Paper;* the resulting paper was called *Frederick Douglass's Paper.* In 1858, Douglass began publishing *Douglass's Monthly* for British readers. The weekly ran until 1860; he stopped printing the monthly in 1863, thus ending a 16-year publishing career.

Douglass served as a Rochester stationmaster on the underground railroad. He hid hundreds of escaping slaves at the *North Star* printing office and at his home. He made arrangements for them to travel to Canada.

In January 1871, President Grant appointed Douglass to a commission to Santo Domingo (Dominican Republic). He moved to Washington, D.C., because he thought that more federal appointments would be offered. In 1877, President Rutherford Hayes appointed him United States Marshal for the District of Columbia. He served in that position until 1881, when President James Garfield appointed him Recorder of Deeds for the District of Columbia. He held that office until 1886.

In September 1889, President Benjamin Harrison appointed Douglass Minister-Resident and Consul-General to the Republic of Haiti, where he served until July 1891. Douglass, one of the strongest antislavery voices of his time, died of a heart attack in Washington, D.C., on February 20, 1895. Douglass was motivated for his entire adult life to work for the civil rights cause.

ELIZABETH BLACKWELL—First U.S. Woman Doctor

"We may forget the early struggles of the doctors Elizabeth and Emily Blackwell, but what we should never forget is that the dignity, the culture, and the high moral standards which formed their character, finally prevailed in overcoming the existing prejudice, both within and outside the profession. By their standards, the status of women in medicine was determined."

Dr. Elizabeth Cushier

Elizabeth Blackwell's desire to become a medical doctor did not develop slowly. It occurred as a significant emotional event in her early 20s while visiting a friend who was dying of cancer. Blackwell considered the study of medicine. Although she had been content with her social and family life, it was not a fulfilling life for her. She did not feel challenged.

Blackwell entered her personal reflections on pursuing the study of medicine in her diary. "The idea of winning a doctor's degree gradually assumed the aspect of a great moral struggle, and the moral fight possessed an immense attraction for me. This work has taken deep root in my soul and become an all-absorbing duty. I must accomplish my end. I consider it the noblest and most useful path that I can tread." Blackwell sent out applications to medical schools while teaching to earn money for tuition. She wanted to attend medical school in Philadelphia, which she considered the medical center of the United States because of its four highly regarded medical schools.

Blackwell sent her first inquiry to Dr. Joseph Warrington in Philadelphia. His response was discouraging; he viewed men as doctors and women as nurses and recommended that she pursue a nursing career. However, he added: "if the project be of divine origin and appointment, it will sooner or later surely be accomplished." She applied to 29 medical schools for admission and received 28 rejections. In late October 1847, Blackwell received an acceptance from the medical school of Geneva College, Geneva, New York. The president of Geneva College was an open-minded individual who had recruited an extremely capable dean for the medical school, Dr. Charles Lee.

The circumstances surrounding Blackwell's acceptance were unusual. Dr. Warrington wrote a letter to Dr. Lee on her behalf. The Geneva faculty was unanimously against the admission of a woman to their medical school. However, they did not want to be responsible for rejecting the highly regarded Philadelphia doctor's request. The faculty turned the decision over to the medical students; they were confident that the students would vote against her admission.

Dr. Lee read Dr. Warrington's letter to the class and informed them that the faculty would let the students determine the issue. He told them that one negative vote would prevent Blackwell's admission. The students were enthusiastic about her admittance, and the single dissenting student was browbeaten into submission. She received a document composed by the students and signed by the chairman of the class, as noted by Peggy Chambers in *A Doctor Alone, A Biography of Elizabeth Blackwell:*

> Resolved—That one of the radical principles of a Republican Government is the universal education of both sexes; that to every branch of scientific education the door should be open equally to all; that the application of Elizabeth Blackwell to become a member of our class meets our entire approbation; and in extending our unanimous invitation we pledge ourselves that no conduct of ours shall cause her to regret her attendance at this institution.

Blackwell was overjoyed to receive the acceptance. She was not sure what to expect from her fellow medical students; however, she had grown up with brothers and was not an overly sensitive young woman. The Geneva community was not ready for a female medical student, and, initially, she had difficulty finding a place to live. She moved into a drafty attic room in a boarding house.

Eventually, Blackwell became aware that she was being subjected to a form of ostracism. The other boarders were unfriendly at mealtime, the women she passed on the street held their skirts to one side and did not speak, and one doctor's wife snubbed her openly. Although her feelings were hurt by this treatment, she reacted by staying in her room and studying.

Blackwell's professor of anatomy was Dr. James Webster, who was friendly and sincerely glad to have her in his class. He predicted: "You'll go through the course and get your diploma—with great éclat too. We'll give you the opportunities. You'll make a stir, I can tell you."

However, within a short time, Dr. Webster prevented Blackwell from attending a dissection. He wrote a note to her explaining that he was about to lecture on the reproductive organs and that he could not cover the material satisfactorily in the presence of a lady. He offered her the opportunity for dissection and study of this portion of the course in private. She knew that Dr. Webster had a reputation for being coarse in covering this material. He sprinkled his lecture with humorous anecdotes. The students liked this approach to the subject matter and responded by becoming somewhat rowdy.

Blackwell replied to Dr. Webster, reminding him that she was a student with a serious purpose, and that she was aware of his awkward position, particularly "when viewed from the low standpoint of impure and unchaste sentiments." She asked why a student of science would have his mind diverted from such an absorbing subject by the presence of a student in feminine attire. She offered to remove her bonnet and sit in the back row of benches, but if the class wished she would not attend the class.

Dr. Webster acquiesced, and Blackwell attended the dissection, which was "just about as much as I could bear." She noted in her diary: "My delicacy was certainly shocked, and yet the exhibition was in some sense ludicrous. I had to pinch my hand until the blood nearly came, and call on Christ to help me from smiling, for that would have ruined everything; but I sat in grave indifference, though the effort made my heart palpitate most painfully."

Blackwell considered how to spend the summer adding to her medical knowledge. One of the few places open to her was Blockley Almshouse in Philadelphia, which cared for 2,000 lower-class unfortunates. Again, Blackwell had to pay for being a pioneer. The resident doctors snubbed her and left a ward when she entered it. They neglected to enter the diagnosis and the notation of the medication used in treatment on the patients' charts. She had to make many of her own diagnoses. Her major accomplishment that summer was the preparation of a thesis on typhus for which she received compliments from senior staff physicians.

Blackwell worked hard during her second year of medical school. Although she had always received good grades, she approached her final exams with trepidation. When the results were compiled, Elizabeth had the best academic record in the class. However, the administration of Geneva College vacillated on establishing the precedent of awarding the first medical degree to a woman in the United States.

Dr. Webster defended her, saying, "She paid her tuition didn't she? She passed every course, each and every one with honors! And let me tell you, gentlemen, if you hold back, I'll take up a campaign in every medical journal." Blackwell received her medical degree on January 23, 1849. Her brother, Henry, traveled to Geneva to share the experience with her. He documented his recollections of the ceremony, as quoted by Ishbel Ross in *Child of Destiny:*

> He [Dr. Lee, who gave the valedictory address] pronounced her the leader of the class; stated that she had passed through a thorough course in every department, slighting none; that she had profited to the utmost by all the advantages of the institution, and by her ladylike and dignified deportment had proved that the strongest intellect and nerve, and the most untiring perseverance were compatible with the softest attributes of feminine delicacy and grace, to all which the students manifested, by decided attempts at applause, their entire concurrence.

As Blackwell left the ceremony, the women of Geneva displayed their smiles and friendly faces to her. She was pleased to see this change in attitude; however, she recorded her true feelings in her diary: "For the next few hours, before I left by train, my room was thronged by visitors. I was glad of the sudden conversion thus shown, but my past experience had given me a useful and permanent lesson at the outset of life as to the very shallow nature of popularity."

Blackwell returned to Philadelphia with the hope of being accepted by the medical community there. She attended lectures at the University of Pennsylvania, but it was obvious that she was not going to be given the opportunity to gain the practical medical experience she needed. She obtained that experience at St. Bartholomew's Hospital in London and at La Maternite in Paris. Again, she encountered bias. She was not given access to all departments at St. Bartholomew's, and at La Maternite, she was considered an aide, not a doctor.

Upon Blackwell's return to New York, she was unable to find a position at the city dispensaries and hospitals. She opened her own dispensary. She lectured on women's health subjects and published two books.

On May 12, 1857, Blackwell opened the New York Infirmary for Women and Children. Charles A. Dana, Cyrus W. Field, and Horace Greeley were trustees of the infirmary. In 1868, Blackwell opened her medical college. For 31 years, the college filled a need in providing medical education for women. In 1899, it was incorporated into the Cornell Medical Center. The infirmary founded by Elizabeth Blackwell is now part of New York Infirmary—Beekman Downtown Hospital.

In 1899, Hobart and William Smith Colleges, successors to Geneva College, named its first residence hall for women Blackwell House. Elizabeth Blackwell was a pioneer who encountered many obstacles. She was sufficiently motivated to overcome them and to make significant contributions to the medical profession.

* * *

Douglass and Blackwell were highly motivated individuals—Douglass as a speaker and editor for the civil rights cause and Blackwell in finally accomplishing a goal that she had set in her youth. Douglass overcame widespread prejudice and even physical injury. Blackwell was scorned and received little support in ultimately achieving her goal in life: becoming a medical doctor.

CHAPTER 9

ASSERTIVENESS—ROLE MODELS

Thomas J. Watson (1874-1956) Founder of IBM

Steve Jobs (1955-2011) Founder of Apple Computer

"Assertiveness is the ability to maintain our boundaries and express our needs clearly and directly. It includes being able to express emotions that we are feeling and offer opinions that may be unpopular or run counter to the 'group think.' Although being assertive means asking for what we want, it does not mean that we always get what we ask for. Assertiveness has gotten a bad rap in society because it is often confused with aggression."

Harvey Deutschendorf, *The Other Kind of Smart*

THOMAS J. WATSON—Founder of IBM Corporation

"Within us all there are wells of thought and dynamics of energy which are not suspected until emergencies arise. Then oftentimes we find that it is comparatively simple to double or treble our former capacities and to amaze ourselves by the results achieved. Quotas, when set for us by others, are challenges which goad us on to surpass ourselves. The outstanding leaders of every age are those who set up their own quotas and constantly exceed them. The great accomplishments of man have resulted from the transmission of ideas and enthusiasm."

Thomas J. Watson

Thomas J. Watson, founder of the IBM Corporation, was born on February 17, 1874, in Campbell, New York. Watson enrolled at the Miller School of Commerce in Elmira, and, in May 1892, completed the accounting and business program. He accepted a position as a bookkeeper, but soon decided that "I couldn't sit on a high stool and keep books all my life." He formed opinions early about what he didn't want to do, but he wasn't yet sure what he wanted to do.

A neighbor of the Watsons operated a hardware store and consignment business. He acquired organs, pianos, and sewing machines and sold them on consignment from a wagon. Watson went on the road selling for him; it was the first of his many sales jobs. Watson learned the importance of a neat appearance and of making a good first impression. He sold for the neighbor for two years without a raise and without many kind words of encouragement from him. His boss was astounded when Watson quit after two years. Only then did he offer Watson a raise; he even offered to sell him the business.

Watson applied for a job with the National Cash Register Company (NCR) and met the manager of the Buffalo office. The manager wasn't interested in hiring him, but Watson persuaded the manager to offer him a job. Watson made no sales during the first two weeks, and the manager made his disappointment clear. Watson absorbed his constructive criticism and, within a year, was one of the most successful NCR salesmen in the East. By the time he was 25, Watson was the top salesman in the Buffalo office.

John Henry Patterson, chief executive officer of NCR, made the cash register virtually indispensible to businessmen and then monopolized its manufacture and distribution. Patterson was a successful manager because he combined paternalism with an emphasis on training. He realized that salesmen responded to the fear of punishment and the promise of reward. Patterson knew just how hard he could push Watson. He became the shaper of Watson's life over the next 11 years.

In the summer of 1899, Patterson promoted Watson to manager of the Rochester office. Watson moved the sales of the Rochester branch from near the bottom of all NCR's offices to sixth from the top within several months. He was assertive in beating his main competitor, the Hallwood Company, and his performance was followed closely by Hugh Chalmers, NCR's general manager, and by Patterson.

NCR had between 80 and 95 percent of the sales of new cash registers. Patterson decided to be aggressive in reducing the impact of sales of used cash registers. Patterson gave Watson $1 million to set up a company to front for NCR in driving out used cash register competition in the United States.

Watson established Watson's Cash Register and Second Hand Exchange in Manhattan, undercut the prices of his main competitor, and bought him out. He repeated this activity in Philadelphia and Chicago. He made the second-hand machine business a profitable unit of NCR and was offered a position at the headquarters in Dayton.

Eventually, Chalmers could no longer tolerate Patterson's dictatorial style, and, as the number two man in NCR, he disagreed with some of Patterson's non-business decisions. Chalmers was fired; Watson was promoted to general manager in his place. Patterson went to Europe for two years, and, by the time he returned, Watson had doubled the sales volume (to 100,000 cash registers in 1910).

NCR management's monopolistic practices in the second-hand cash register business caught up with them. On February 22, 1913, Patterson, Watson, and 28 other company managers were indicted on three counts of criminal conspiracy and were placed on trial in Cincinnati for restraining trade and maintaining a monopoly.

Patterson, Watson, and all but one of the other senior NCR managers were found guilty as charged. Patterson and Watson were released on bail. Watson was fired, just as Chalmers had been abruptly dismissed earlier.

Watson received a job offer from Charles Flint, who had assembled a company called the Computer-Tabulating-Recording Company (CTR) by combining a computing scales company, a time recorder company, and the Tabulating Machine Company. CTR was unprofitable, and Flint wanted a new manager. Watson accepted Flint's offer; however, he wasn't elected to the board of directors because of the pending NCR lawsuit. On March 13, 1915, the District Court verdict was set aside and a new trial granted. No new trial was conducted, and Watson was cleared of any wrongdoing. CTR promptly elected Watson president and general manager.

Watson authorized the redesign of the Hollerith (punched card) tabulator, and the Tabulating Machine Company became the premier unit of CTR.

In 1924, Watson renamed the company International Business Machines (IBM). He was appointed chief executive officer and, for the first time, was really in charge of the company.

Unlike many companies, IBM expanded during the Great Depression. By 1940, IBM was still small ($50 million sales per year), but it had become the largest company in the office equipment industry, due largely to Watson's assertive management. World War II made IBM a large company. From 1939 to 1945, gross income increased from $40 million to $140 million. By 1949, the company was five times larger than it had been in 1939.

In 1952, Watson's son, Thomas J. Watson, Jr., became president of IBM. From 1914 through 1953, assets had been multiplied by 24, employees by 34, the data processing business by 316, and development expenditures by 500. On May 8, 1956, Thomas J. Watson, Jr., became chief executive officer of the IBM Corporation. Just over a month later, on June 19, Thomas J. Watson, Sr., died of a heart attack.

STEVE JOBS—Founder of Apple Computer

"His tenacity is what makes him great. Several years after leaving Steve's employ, Susan Barnes conducted a study about family run businesses. She found that the key to success was 'pure staying power, persistence, continually believing in something, doggedness to get things done, and continual optimism.' That was a good description of Steve Jobs. Steve was beaten down many times but 'he kept getting off the mat,' she says."

Alan Deutschman, *The Second Coming of Steve Jobs*

Steve Jobs was one of the first to envision that people would buy a computer for their home because they wanted to do some business tasks or to run educational applications for themselves or their children. Furthermore, he foresaw the need to link the home with a "nationwide communications network," the Internet.

Jobs became interested in electronics at the age of 10. Many Hewlett-Packard engineers lived in his neighborhood in Mountain View, California, and he was intrigued with many electronics projects assembled in neighborhood garages. One neighbor instructed Jobs in electronics and enrolled him in the Hewlett-Packard Explorer Club, where he learned about calculators, diodes, holograms, and lasers.

Jobs's first project for the Explorer Club was building a frequency counter. He needed parts and obtained them with the assertiveness for which he became known. He looked up Bill Hewlett in the Palo Alto phone book. Hewlett answered the phone and talked with Jobs for 20 minutes. He not only gave Jobs the parts he needed but also gave him a summer job at Hewlett-Packard assembling frequency counters. Later, when Jobs needed another part, he called the Burroughs Corporation in Detroit collect, and asked them to donate it.

Jobs's future partner, Steve Wozniak, was only 19 when he met Jobs, but his knowledge of electronics was advanced for his age. He had won prizes in local electronics fairs against tough competition.

Wozniak dropped out of Berkeley during his junior year and accepted a position as an engineer in Hewlett-Packard's calculator division. He became a regular attendee at meetings of the Homebrew Computer Club, a gathering place for computer hobbyists, engineers, programmers, and suppliers.

Attendance at club meetings increased exponentially after the January 1975 issue of *Popular Electronics* was circulated. It included an article about the Altair 8800 computer kit produced by MITS in Albuquerque, New Mexico. The Altair central processing unit used an Intel 8080 microprocessor. The Altair was a collection of parts with meager documentation and little input / output capability. Orders from hobbyists for this first mail-order computer overwhelmed MITS. BASIC programming language for the Intel 8080 was developed by Bill Gates and Paul Allen, who later founded Microsoft Corporation.

Wozniak designed his own computer. He took his computer to meetings of the Homebrew Computer Club, but they were not interested in it because it was not based on the integrated circuit used in the Altair. He offered to give away circuit diagrams of his computer to club members, but Jobs suggested that they sell them. Better yet, Jobs suggested that they make the circuit-board computers and sell them. On April 1, 1976, Jobs and Wozniak formed a partnership called Apple Computer to make and sell computers. Jobs developed a reputation as a tough negotiator. He was called "the rejector," because he usually turned down early designs and estimates.

Jobs met an electronics retailer at a Homebrew Club meeting who offered to buy 50 circuit-board computers, called Apple I. Apple Computer needed start-up capital to build them, but no one was willing to lend it to them. Jobs's loan requests were turned down by banks and by his previous employer at an electronics warehouse store. Finally, Jobs found a supplier of electronics parts in Palo Alto who would sell them parts on credit with no interest if they paid within 30 days. When Wozniak designed the next generation computer, Jobs contracted out the insertion of components into circuit boards. The company he chose did not want the work, but Jobs succeeded with his assertive "I'm not going to leave here until you agree" approach.

Until this time in his life, Jobs had been an individual in search of a cause. In promoting the personal computer, he had found his cause. He had a knack for convincing talented people to undertake projects for Apple.

One of Jobs's important early decisions was his choice of an advertising / public relations firm. He was referred to the Regis McKenna Agency. McKenna turned him down. Again Jobs asserted himself; he called McKenna three or four times a day until he agreed to take on Apple as a client.

The fledgling enterprise needed capital to expand. Mike Markkula was recommended as the venture capitalist. Markkula offered to devote four years to Apple and provide money to develop and manufacture the Apple II in return for a one-third ownership in the company. On January 3, 1977, Apple Computer Company was incorporated.

Apple II, because of Wozniak's original design and Jobs's efforts as "rejector," was a work of art. It was easy to produce and it looked good when the cover was raised. Jobs negotiated bargain-basement prices for Apple's components.

In early 1977, Apple II was demonstrated in an attention-gathering booth at a computer fair in San Francisco. Thirteen thousand attendees were captivated by Apple II, and 300 orders were placed. Markkula worked hard to obtain additional capital to fuel Apple's growth. He was amazingly successful.

Apple's next product was an enhanced Apple II, Apple III. In addition to enhancements, the company provided improvements that customers and dealers had requested. Sales of Apple III were less than forecasted. Fortunately, sales of Apple II, which had little competition in 1979, were strong.

Following Apple III's limited success, Jobs needed a new goal. He sought a partner; he considered IBM and Xerox despite the fact that Apple considered IBM the enemy.

Xerox had invested in Apple's second private investment placement. Jobs contacted the Xerox Development Corporation, the company's venture capital unit, and offered to let them invest in Apple if they would give him a tour of their Palo Alto Research Center (PARC). PARC had a talented staff of computer scientists who had made many breakthroughs that Xerox had failed to exploit. Xerox purchased 100,000 shares of Apple at $10.00 and opened their doors to Jobs. The 25-year-old entrepreneur had gotten his way again.

Larry Tesler of PARC demonstrated their Alto personal computer to Jobs and seven Apple developers, who were enthusiastic when they saw the Alto's potential. User interaction with the Alto was revolutionary through the use of icons, menus (action lists), partitions of the screen (windows), and a "mouse." Jobs was moved by what he saw. He shouted: "Why aren't you doing anything with this? This is the greatest thing! This is revolutionary!" After the demonstration, Jobs hired Tesler to work for Apple. Later, Alan Kay, one of PARC's principal computer science visionaries, joined Apple and eventually became an Apple Fellow.

In August 1980, Markkula reorganized Apple into three divisions. Jobs had hoped to be given line authority of a division; instead, he was named Chairman of the Board. On December 12, 1980, Apple Computer Corporation went public. Apple's shares sold out within the first hour.

In 1981, Wozniak crashed his Beechcraft Bonanza light plane and underwent a long recuperation period. He did not return to Apple full time. Jobs and Wozniak made significant contributions to the computer industry. They succeeded where large corporations failed; they pioneered the personal computer revolution. In 1985, President Reagan awarded National Technology Medals to Jobs and Wozniak at the White House.

Without line responsibility in the reorganization of Apple, Jobs was again without a project. He needed a subject for his evangelism. The Macintosh personal computer was the next project to provide an outlet for his zeal. Macintosh was in the R & D phase. Developers planned a "luggable" machine that would be easy to use and would sell for about $1,000. Hardware and software designers would work together from the beginning, and software would be offered as part of the purchase price of the machine. Jobs took over the project and brought in developers from the successful Apple II. Jobs headed the Macintosh Division when it was formed.

Markkula was in a difficult position because his four-year arrangement with Apple was almost over. He looked outside Apple for a new president. He wanted John Sculley, President of Pepsi-Cola USA, who had taken market share from Coca-Cola. Initially, Sculley was not interested in joining Apple. Jobs flew to New York City and courted Sculley. After many long conversations about the future of Apple, Jobs asked Sculley if he intended to sell sugar water to children for the rest of his life when he could be doing something important with personal computers.

Sculley accepted the presidency of Apple and spent many hours learning the technology. Within his first year on the job, he realized that cuts would have to be made. Apple II was carrying the company. He streamlined the organizational structure and eliminated 1,200 jobs to keep the company profitable. Jobs retained his position as manager of the Macintosh Division in addition to serving as Chairman of the Board. Sculley redirected the company from producing most of its own software to increased reliance on outside software developers.

The first disagreements between Jobs and Sculley occurred in 1983. By 1984, when Macintosh sales were considerably below Jobs's estimates, the rift was obvious to everyone. Apple lowered the price of Macintosh, but sales continued to be disappointing. At the Board meeting on April 11, 1985, Sculley dismissed Jobs as manager of the Macintosh Division. Jobs then attempted to have Sculley removed as president and CEO. However, he misjudged Sculley's support from the Board of Directors. Finally, their disagreements became so disruptive that the Board suggested that Sculley force Jobs out of the company.

Jobs founded NeXT, a computer company that produced an expensive computer for academic users. Tim Berners-Lee invented the World Wide Web on a NeXT computer. Nevertheless, it had a limited market, so NeXT concentrated on software development. Jobs then founded Pixar, which produced computer-automated cartoons, such as the highly profitable *Toy Story*.

In 1996, Apple bought NeXT to use its software as the foundation for the next-generation MAC operating system. NeXT software became the basis for all future Apple operating systems. Jobs came with the purchase of NeXT. In 1997, Apple's sales and earnings plummeted, and Jobs was appointed interim CEO and led Apple's rebound. He became CEO in 2000.

In 2001, Apple introduced the iPod and became a consumer electronics company and the major company in the media-player market. In 2007, Jobs announced the iPhone, a powerful pocket-sized personal computer, which incorporated a new touch screen and interface and dominated the smart phone market. In 2010, the iPad, a highly successful tablet computer, was introduced by Apple.

In his personal life, Jobs was diagnosed in 2004 with a rare form of pancreatic cancer that could be controlled. He underwent surgery and returned to work.

In 2005, Jobs gave the commencement address at Stanford University. He said, "Your time is limited, so don't waste it living someone else's life. Don't be trapped by dogma, which is living with the results of someone else's thinking. Don't let the noise of others' opinions drown out your own inner voice. And most important, have the courage to follow your heart and intuition. They somehow already know what you truly want to become. Everything else is secondary."

In 2009, Jobs received a liver transplant. He again returned to work. On August 24, 2011, Jobs turned over his CEO responsibilities to Tim Cook, the Chief Operating Officer. Jobs died from complications of pancreatic cancer on October 5, 2011.

In 2011, Apple's market capitalization exceeded that of ExxonMobil, making it the world's most valuable company. Jobs revitalized six industries: personal computers, animated movies, music, telephones, tablet computing, and digital publishing. He also had a significant impact on retailing with the establishment of the Apple retail stores.

Jobs, who considered himself an artist, had a passion for design. He combined art, technology, and ease of use in his products. Jobs did no market research. He did not ask customers what they wanted; rather, he gave them what he thought they should have.

Steve Jobs was the greatest business executive of the late twentieth and early twenty-first centuries. It is thought that historians will rank him with Henry Ford and Thomas Edison.

* * *

Watson and Jobs were assertive individuals, a quality that contributed heavily to their success in industry. However, Jobs was in a class by himself in getting people to do what they didn't want to do.

CHAPTER 10

RELATIONSHIPS—ROLE MODELS

Elizabeth Cady Stanton (1815-1902) Women's Rights Policy Maker

Susan B. Anthony (1820-1906) Women's Rights Organizer

"The art of relationships is, in large part, skill in managing emotions in others. Social competence and incompetence, and the specific skills involved . . . are the abilities that undergrid popularity, leadership, and interpersonal effectiveness. People who do well in these skills do well at anything that relies on interacting smoothly with others; they are the social stars. . . . Talent, that of empathy and connecting . . . makes it easy to enter into an encounter or to recognize and respond fittingly to people's feelings and concerns—the art of relationship. Such people make good 'team players.'"

Daniel Goleman, *Emotional Intelligence: Why It Can Matter More Than IQ*

ELIZABETH CADY STANTON—Women's Rights Policy Maker

"Stanton's talents were aptly suited to the role of agitator. Well educated and widely read, she had keen intelligence, a trained mind, and an ability to argue persuasively in writing and speaking. Her personality was magnetic. In conversation and correspondence she was willful and opinionated; in person, she was funny, feisty, engaging. Her most remarkable trait was her self-confidence. It gave her the courage to take controversial stands without hesitation."

Elizabeth Griffith, *In Her Own Right: The Life of Elizabeth Cady Stanton*

The conditions that confronted women in the United States in the mid-nineteenth century are difficult to envision today. Women weren't allowed to vote. A college education was denied them. Women couldn't own property, and any wages they earned were turned over to their husbands. The guardianship of children was automatically given to the father in cases of separation and divorce. By law, a woman's inheritance went to her husband. She wasn't entitled to the rights given to the least responsible men, whether they were born in the United States or were immigrants.

Elizabeth Cady Stanton was a leader in the Women's Rights Movement for over 50 years. In order to appreciate her role and her contribution to the movement, it is important to understand her relationship with two other leaders of the movement, Lucretia Mott and Susan B. Anthony. Cady Stanton met Lucretia Mott at the World Anti-Slavery Convention in London in 1840. Mott, a Quaker minister and a reformer active in both the abolitionist and temperance movements, was 22 years older than Cady Stanton and became her mentor.

Cady Stanton and Mott "resolved to hold a convention as soon as they returned home and to form a society to advocate the rights of women." However, the first Women's Rights Convention in the United States wasn't convened until eight years later in Seneca Falls, New York, on July 19 and 20, 1848. The *Declaration of Sentiments*, written by Cady Stanton, was based on the *Declaration of Independence*. The *Declaration of Sentiments*, as adopted at the convention, asserted that "all men and women are created equal."

Elizabeth Cady Stanton and Susan B. Anthony met three years later, in March 1851, after an antislavery meeting in Seneca Falls. Anthony never married and was less of an extrovert than Cady Stanton. Cady Stanton's and Anthony's abilities complemented each other extremely well. Cady Stanton was the policy formulator, effective writer, and movingly expressive speechmaker; Anthony's strengths were her organizational ability and her willingness to campaign and make campaign arrangements.

Cady Stanton's first encounter with activists was with abolitionists whom she met at the home of her cousin, Gerrit Smith, in Peterboro, New York. Smith was a political reformer and staunch antislavery activist. Elizabeth met and fell in love with Henry Stanton, a well-known abolitionist, on one of her visits to Peterboro. Henry was a dynamic individual and a powerful, effective speaker. They met in October 1839, when Henry spoke at local antislavery meetings; he was an agent of the American Anti-Slavery Society and secretary of the national society. After a brief courtship, Elizabeth and Henry were married in Johnstown, New York, on May 1, 1840.

Cady Stanton and Henry left for New York City after the wedding to travel to London for the World Anti-Slavery Convention, where Cady Stanton met Lucretia Mott. The convention wasn't a success; agreement wasn't reached on any of its goals. However, it did plant the seed for the Women's Rights Movement in the United States by providing the occasion for two of its leaders to meet.

Mott encouraged Cady Stanton to think independently about religion and individual rights: "When I first heard from her lips that I had the same right to think for myself that Luther, Calvin, and John Knox had, and the same right to be guided by my own convictions, I felt a newborn sense of dignity and freedom."

When the Stantons returned home, Henry read law with Judge Cady in Johnstown for the next 15 months. In late 1842, Henry joined a law practice in Boston. In 1843, Cady Stanton moved to Boston and found it a stimulating city. William Lloyd Garrison and many strong-willed abolitionists lived there, and it was, generally, a home for liberal thinkers. The Stantons entertained frequently; their guests included Ralph Waldo Emerson, Stephen Foster, Nathaniel Hawthorne, James Russell Lowell, and John Greenleaf Whittier.

The Stantons were happy in Boston, but Henry developed a chronic lung congestion and needed a less humid climate. In 1847, they moved to Seneca Falls, New York, where Henry resumed the practice of law.

In March 1848, the New York Married Women's Property Act was passed by the legislature; New York was the first State to pass a bill of this type. The bill, which ensured that married women could hold the title to property in their own names, was first introduced to the legislature in 1836 but didn't pass at the time. Cady Stanton had circulated petitions in support of the bill and had lobbied for its passage with members of the Legislature.

Cady Stanton had difficulty adjusting to the small-town atmosphere of Seneca Falls after the dynamic social and political scene in Boston. The demands of her young, growing family weighed upon her. Henry was busy with his career and was out of town frequently on trips to Albany and Washington. She was pleased to hear that Mott planned to visit Waterloo, just west of Seneca Falls, in July 1848.

Cady Stanton was invited to spend July 13 with Mott at the home of Jane and Richard Hunt in Waterloo. Mott's sister, Martha Wright of Auburn, and Mary M'Clintock were also there that day; all five women were eager to proceed with the conference that Mott and Cady Stanton had discussed eight years previously. Cady Stanton remembered that she "poured . . . out the torrent of my long-accumulating discontent with such violence and indignation that I stirred myself, as well as the rest of the party, to do and dare anything."

The women called a convention for July 19 and 20 at the Wesleyan Chapel in Seneca Falls. A notice appeared in the *Seneca County Courier* on July 14 announcing a "convention to discuss the social, civil, and religious condition and rights of women." All of these women, the nucleus of the convention, were married and had children. All but Cady Stanton were staunch antislavery activists. Mott was the only one of the five who had any experience as a delegate, orator, or organizer. However, all of them had attended temperance and antislavery conventions.

Cady Stanton's *Declaration of Sentiments*, essentially a declaration of women's rights, was the principal document reviewed at the convention and the basis for the resolutions that were passed. Over

100 men and women were present each day. The clause requesting women's right to vote wasn't universally accepted. Both Lucretia Mott and Henry Stanton were against its inclusion in the *Declaration of Sentiments*, but Cady Stanton prevailed; it was left in.

The convention was successful, and a number of resolutions were passed including the following:

- Resolved, that all laws which prevent woman from occupying such a station in society as her conscience shall dictate, or which place her in a position inferior to that of man, are contrary to the great precept of nature, and there fore of no force or authority. . . .

- Resolved, that woman is man's equal—was intended to be so by the creator, and the highest good of the human race demands that she should be recognized as such. . . .

- Resolved, that it is the duty of the women of this country to secure themselves their sacred right to the elective franchise. . . .

Some newspaper columnists ridiculed the convention; other editors were sympathetic to the women's cause. Frederick Douglass, writing in the *North Star*, saw no reason to deny women the right to vote because "right is of no sex." The convention was the beginning of the Women's Rights Movement in the United States.

In 1854, Cady Stanton spoke to the New York State Legislature about the need for improvements to the married women's property law. She reviewed the *Declaration of Sentiments*, and discussed the lack of the women's rights to vote, to hold office, to earn wages, and to inherit from their families.

Stanton's speech included a plea for women to be able to own property, to be guardians for their own children, and to be eligible for higher education. She made a strong, favorable impression on the Legislature. In 1860, the New York State Legislature passed a law granting women the right to earn and keep their own wages and to be custodians for their own children.

In 1869, Cady Stanton and Anthony founded the National Woman Suffrage Association; Cady Stanton was elected president, and Anthony was elected secretary. Cady Stanton held this position for 21 years. However, Cady Stanton's strong stands on women's rights weren't for everyone. In late 1869, conservative suffragists who disagreed with Cady Stanton formed a rival organization, the American Woman Suffrage Association. This competing organization was comprised mainly of New Englanders led by Lucy Stone.

In 1888, Cady Stanton convinced Senator Aaron Sargent to introduce a women's suffrage amendment as a supplement to the Fifteenth Amendment to the Constitution. It failed that year, but it was introduced in every session of Congress until finally adopted in 1920.

In 1890, the two major women's suffrage organizations joined forces. Cady Stanton was elected president, Anthony was elected vice-president, and Stone became head of the executive committee of the combined National American Woman Suffrage Association. Cady Stanton presided over the new organization for two years and then turned over the reins to Anthony.

Cady Stanton never gave up her quest for the right of women to vote. On October 25, 1902, the day before she died, she wrote a letter to President Theodore Roosevelt requesting his support in obtaining the vote for women. In the words of author Ida Husted Harper, "If the intellect of Elizabeth Cady Stanton had been possessed by a man, he would have had a seat on the Supreme Bench or the Senate of the United States, but our country has no rewards for great women."

Elizabeth Cady Stanton didn't live to see the fruits of her labor. Her efforts weren't completely rewarded until 18 years after her death. In 1920, the Nineteenth Amendment to the Constitution was ratified. It includes the statement that "the right of citizens of the United States to vote shall not be denied or abridged by the United States or by any State on account of sex." All of society, not just women, benefited from Elizabeth Cady Stanton's lifelong struggle for women's rights.

SUSAN B. ANTHONY—Women's Rights Organizer

"Susan B. Anthony became one of the most unconventional women of the nineteenth century. Her life of confrontational political leadership on behalf of her sex provokes a question: If not from personal anguish and rebellion, if not with high political questions, how did a common woman arise and, in Anthony's case, become the most dramatic and charismatic of feminist rebels—known by many as the 'Napoleon' of nineteenth century feminism?"

Kathleen Barry, *Susan B. Anthony: A Biography of a Singular Feminist*

Two weeks after the first Women's Rights Convention on July 19 and 20, 1848, in Seneca Falls, New York, another women's rights convention was held in Rochester. Susan B. Anthony was working in Canajoharie, New York, as the girls' headmistress of the Canajoharie Academy and didn't attend the convention; however, her father, mother, and sister attended and signed petitions in support of the resolutions.

Within two years, Anthony was not only informed about the subject of women's rights, but also had discussed the subject with the abolitionists Frederick Douglass and William Lloyd Garrison, who were promoting the women's rights cause. Her interest in the Women's Rights Movement was sparked by meeting Elizabeth Cady Stanton in 1851 in Seneca Falls, after an antislavery meeting.

It was the beginning of a friendship and a working relationship that was to last for over half a century. Anthony's attention to detail and organizational skills were a perfect match with Cady Stanton's strengths as a philosopher and policy-maker.

In 1852, Anthony attended her first women's rights convention, the third National Women's Rights Convention. Cady Stanton did not attend, because she was at home awaiting the birth of her fifth child. However, she sent a letter for Anthony to read to the convention. Two thousand delegates attended, including Lucretia Mott, James Mott, and Lucy Stone.

The working relationship between Anthony and Cady Stanton was demonstrated by the way they prepared a speech for Stanton to give to the New York State Legislature in February 1854. They addressed the right of women to earn and keep their own wages and the right of women to own property in their name. Cady Stanton was willing to give the speech; however, with her large, young family, she didn't have enough time to prepare it. She sent a plea for help to Anthony, and they arranged to collaborate. Anthony and a lawyer friend would research the laws including discriminating statements against women and assemble the information, if Cady Stanton would write and present the speech.

Cady Stanton's perception of their working relationship is observed by Elizabeth Griffith in *In Her Own Right:*

> In thought and sympathy we were one, and in the division of labor we exactly complemented each other. In writing, we did better work together than either of us could have done alone. I am the better writer, she the better critic. She supplied the facts and statistics, I the philosophy and rhetoric and together we have made arguments that have stood unshaken through the storms of 30 long years. Our speeches may be considered the united product of two brains.

Cady Stanton's speech at Albany provided examples of the ways in which women were discriminated against and the means by which the law could be changed to address the discrimination. Anthony obtained 6,000 signatures on the petitions for women's property and wage reform and 4,000 signatures on the petition in support of women's right to vote. Changes to the laws on women's property and wage reform wouldn't come for another six years in New York. When the changes came, Cady Stanton and Anthony knew that they had played a key role in making those changes.

The Fifteenth Amendment to the Constitution, which was adopted in 1870, includes a statement that "the right of citizens of the United States to vote shall not be denied . . . on account of race, color, or previous condition of servitude." The suffragists wanted the phrase "or sex" to be included in the Fifteenth Amendment. However, the phrase wasn't included, so women began to test the interpretation of their rights as citizens implied by the Fifteenth Amendment. Anthony wasn't the first woman to test this interpretation of the Amendment, but she certainly received more news coverage than any other woman.

On November 1, 1872, Anthony attempted to register to vote. The election judges told her that, according to New York State law, she wouldn't be permitted to register. Anthony quoted to them from the amendments to the Constitution and insisted that she, as a citizen, had the right to vote. She was permitted to register, and she voted in the general election on November 5. She received wide newspaper coverage, including articles in the *Chicago Tribune* and the *New York Times*. She realized that she may have broken the law, and that she might be liable for a $500 fine. On November 18, a marshal came to Anthony's home and arrested her.

Anthony was arraigned, and her bond was set at $500. She refused to pay it, so her lawyer, Henry Selden, who didn't want to see his client go to jail, paid her bail. Unfortunately, by posting the bail for her, he had, inadvertently, prevented her from appealing to higher courts—potentially as high as the Supreme Court; posting bail indicated that she wasn't contesting the lawfulness of her arrest. Anthony made many speeches describing her circumstances, including speeches in Monroe County, where her case was to be tried. The trial was moved to Ontario County, south of Rochester, which was considered a more neutral venue.

On June 17, 1873, Anthony's trial began in Canandaigua, the county seat of Ontario County. The judge selected to try her case was Judge Ward Hunt, an inexperienced judge recently appointed to the bench. Selden conducted a skillful defense, pointing out that Anthony sincerely believed that she had been given the right to vote by the the Fourteenth and Fifteenth Amendments. Judge Hunt refused to let her speak in her own defense.

Judge Hunt stated that it didn't matter what Anthony's beliefs were; she had broken the law. He took a note from his pocket, turned toward the jury, and read from it. The note concluded with the statement, "If I am right in this, the result must be a verdict . . . of guilty and I therefore direct that you find a verdict of guilty." An incensed Selden reminded the judge that he didn't have the right to provide that type of instruction to the jury and demanded that the jury be asked for their verdict. Judge Hunt ignored Selden, instructed the court clerk to record the verdict, and dismissed the jury.

This blatant injustice was widely covered by the press. Many who disapproved of Anthony's voting now sided with her because of this unjust treatment in the courtroom. Judge Hunt's actions were politically motivated. His mentor was Roscoe Conkling, U.S. Senator from New York and a known foe of the Women's Rights Movement. Selden requested a new trial on the basis that Anthony had been denied the right to a fair trial by jury. Judge Hunt denied the request and stated her sentence, a $100 fine. Anthony responded, "I shall never pay a dollar of your unjust penalty."

Anthony never retired from her lifelong effort to promote women's rights. The International Woman Suffrage Alliance was formed in 1904, and Anthony, at the age of 84, was recognized as their leader. At their convention in 1906, she instructed the delegates: "The fight must not stop. You must see that it doesn't stop." At a dinner in her honor in Washington, D.C., on her 86th birthday, she concluded her comments by stating, "Failure is impossible." Susan B. Anthony died on March 13, 1906.

In 1920, the Nineteenth Amendment to the Constitution was ratified. It included the statement that "the right of citizens of the United States to vote shall not be denied or abridged by the United States or by any State on account of sex." It was called the "Susan B. Anthony Amendment." Anthony was right; failure was impossible. She was honored further in 1976 by the United States Government with the minting of the Susan B. Anthony dollar.

* * *

Cady Stanton and Anthony were impressive in their working relationship with each other and with others. They were the classic case of complementary strengths. Together they accomplished many times what they could have achieved as individuals.

CHAPTER 11

TEAMWORK — ROLE MODELS

Knute Rockne (1888-1931) Inspirational Football Coach

Winston Churchill (1874-1965) British Prime Minister During World War II

"A person's ability to be interpersonally intelligent is really challenged when it comes to teamwork. All of us are involved in some kind of teamwork, whether at work, with another parent, in a neighborhood group, or in a service organization. Being a part of a team is challenging because you have less personal control over the outcome than you might have in a one-to-one relationship. It's often frustrating since you have fewer opportunities to get your point across and persuade others. Working on a team takes special skills, such as complementing the styles of others, coordinating the efforts of team members without bossing them around, and building consensus."

Mel Silberman, *People Smart*

KNUTE ROCKNE—Inspirational Football Coach

"I don't like to lose and it isn't so much that it is just a football game, but because defeat means the failure to reach your objective. I don't want a football player who doesn't take defeat to heart, who laughs it off with the thought, oh well, there's another Saturday. The trouble in American life today, in business as well as sports, is that too many people are afraid of competition. The result is that in some circles people have come to sneer at success if it costs hard work and training and sacrifice." Knute Rockne, quoted in

Jerry Bronfield, *Rockne: The Man, the Coach, the Legend*

Knute Rockne's won-lost percentage established him as one of the winningest of college football coaches. During a 13-year period that included five undefeated seasons, his teams won 105, lost twelve, and tied five games. He did not invent the forward pass, but he did as much as any coach to make it an integral part of the game of football.

Above all, Rockne was a motivator. He could inspire a subpar team to get the most out of their talents. On many occasions, his teams beat opposing teams who clearly were more talented.

In 1893, the Rockne family moved from Norway to the Logan Square district of Chicago. A heterogeneous melting-pot of many nationalities, the district had many corner lots for football and baseball games.

Knute's parents thought that football was too rough for him, but he was allowed to play baseball. During a fight at a sandlot baseball game, Knute was hit with a baseball bat on the bridge of his nose, changing its shape forever. After that incident, playing baseball was forbidden, and football was allowed. He played on the scrub football team in high school, but he excelled in track.

In 1907, Rockne worked for the U.S. Post Office in Chicago to earn money for college expenses. He ran in track meets for the Illinois Track Club to keep in good physical condition. Two of his track friends were going to Notre Dame University.

In September 1910, Rockne enrolled as a freshman at Notre Dame and worked as a janitor in the chemistry lab. Initially, he played inter-hall football for his dormitory and then became the starting fullback for the freshman football team. When Rockne arrived in South Bend, the Notre Dame varsity football team record was 95 wins, 30 losses, and 10 ties for a .760 winning percentage. They had beaten Michigan and were definitely a team on the rise.

Rockne was the starting left end on the Notre Dame team from 1911 through 1913 and was team captain in his senior year. During his four years at Notre Dame, the varsity football team won 24 games, lost three, and tied one; none of the losses occurred in the three years that Rockne played for the varsity.

During the summer before his senior year, Rockne and the starting quarterback practiced the forward pass in their off hours from their summer jobs. Although the forward pass became legal in 1906, it was little used. When a pass was thrown, the receiver would stop, turn, catch the ball in his chest, and then turn to go downfield. Rockne practiced catching the ball in his hands on the dead run. As a coach, Rockne developed a reputation with pass plays, but he always gave credit to other coaches, including Pop Warner and Amos Alonzo Stagg, for developing the forward pass.

In the fall of 1913, Notre Dame played Army for the first time. The game was played at West Point; the Army team had superior size and was a strong favorite. Army took an early lead with their running game. Rockne, at left end, faked a limp, causing the defensive back covering him to back off. The Notre Dame quarterback hit Rockne with a pass for a touchdown. When Army defended against the pass, the Irish fullback ran through the line. Notre Dame won 35-13, surprising everyone except the victors.

Rockne also ran on the track team, played flute in the college orchestra, boxed in area smokers to earn spending money, and acted in theatrical productions. He majored in pharmacology and chemistry and graduated magna cum laude. Father Julius Nieuwland, professor of chemistry and the inventor of synthetic rubber, considered Rockne his most remarkable student.

After he graduated, Rockne worked as a high school football coach in St. Louis but returned to Notre Dame when offered the positions of instructor in chemistry, assistant football coach, and track coach. Rockne was an assistant coach to football coach Jesse Harper for four years at Notre Dame, which continued to add major schools to its schedule. In the game with Wabash in 1916, Harper was ill, and Rockne was acting head coach. The team experienced for the first time Rockne's pre-game and half-time motivational talks. He concluded by saying, "Now go out there and crucify them." Notre Dame won 60-0.

Rockne's innovations in four years as assistant coach were polishing the backfield shift and "flexing" the ends wider or closer in to the tackles in conjunction with the backfield shift, giving the runner more blockers. Also, he evolved the "boxing tackle" with head feints and diversion of the bulk of the tackle, thus allowing a lighter lineman to handle a heavier tackle. Use of these techniques was called the "Rockne" system or the "Notre Dame" system.

After four years as assistant coach, Rockne felt that he was ready to be a head coach. When Jesse Harper left Notre Dame, he suggested that Rockne replace him as head coach, and the administration agreed.

In the fall of 1916, George Gipp arrived on the Notre Dame campus. After graduating from high school, he had worked in the construction industry and driven a taxi for two years. He had not played football in high school. He was a loner who had difficulty adjusting to college life. Rockne first encountered Gipp on a practice field drop-kicking the football 50 yards, consistently, without much effort. Rockne suggested that he try out for the freshman team; thus began the legend. In his first game, against Western State Normal, Gipp received the call to punt from the quarterback but instead drop-kicked a 62-yard field goal to win the game.

In 1920, late in a game against Indiana, Gipp, with a dislocated shoulder, added to the legend with a slashing touchdown through the line to win the game. In addition to playing in the offensive backfield, Gipp also played defensive back and was the place-kicker / punter. Rockne claimed that no one ever completed a pass in a zone defended by Gipp.

Gipp caught a bad cold and did not start the Northwestern game. After the crowd had called for him for three quarters, he went in and completed his first two passes for touchdowns. However, he was exhausted and had chills. He had to leave the game and was taken to St. Joseph's Hospital, where his condition worsened.

When Gipp lay near death, he told Rockne, "Sometime, Rock, when the team is up against it, when things are wrong, and the breaks are beating the boys—tell them to go in there with all they've got and win just one for the Gipper. I don't know where I'll be then, Rock, but I'll know about it, and I'll be happy." George Gipp died on December 14, 1920 at St. Joseph's Hospital; he was 25 years old. His cold and chronic tonsillitis had led to pneumonia. He died of a streptococcal infection.

Rockne expanded the football schedule. In 1922, Notre Dame played Georgia Tech for the first time. Tech had an excellent team, and the fans in Atlanta intimidated their opponents with rebel yells. In his pre-game pep talk, Rockne read telegrams to the team, including one from the mayor of South Bend and one from the president of the Alumni Association. Finally, Rockne told the team that his four-year-old son was ill and had been taken to the hospital. All of the players knew and loved Billy. Hesitantly, Rockne removed one last telegram from his pocket and read it to the team: "PLEASE WIN THIS GAME FOR MY DADDY. IT IS VERY IMPORTANT TO HIM." Notre Dame won 13-3.

When they returned to South Bend, the usual large crowd at Union Station welcomed the team home. One of the first to greet them was a happy and healthy Billy Rockne, who had not been near a hospital since his birth. Rockne would use any technique to motivate his players. Star running back Jim Crowley explained, as described by Jerry Bronfield in *Rockne:*

> But the guys on the team never considered they'd been taken in by Rock. There wasn't anything to forgive. We were used to Rock's drama—the real and the theatrical—and we'd find out over the next couple of years that Rock would use any ploy he could think of to get the most out of us, whether it was at practice or at a game.

In the fall of 1921, the players who became known as the "four horsemen" entered Notre Dame. The four backs (Jim Crowley, Elmer Layden, Don Miller, and Harry Stuhldreher) were light compared with today's teams, but they had speed and precision. The principal factors in the "Notre Dame shift" were coordination and synchronization. Supposedly, Rockne devised the shift after watching the precision of a line of chorus girls. Plays were rehearsed over and over in slow motion until the backs achieved the necessary precision.

The four horsemen received their name on October 18, 1924, at the Army-Notre Dame game at the Polo Grounds in New York. The student reporter from Notre Dame was seated three feet away from sports writer Grantland Rice in the press box. The previous week, the reporter had seen the movie starring Rudolph Valentino based on *The Four Horsemen of the Apocalypse*. A member of the press observed that the Notre Dame backfield was going to maul Army. The student reporter said, "Just like the four horsemen." Grantland Rice glanced at him and then looked out at the field.

The next day, Grantland Rice reported in the *New York Tribune:* "Outlined against a blue-gray October sky, the Four Horseman rode again. In dramatic lore they were known as Famine, Pestilence, Destruction, and Death. These are only aliases. Their real names are Stuhldreher, Miller, Crowley, and Layden." When the team returned to South Bend, the student reporter told Rockne that he wanted to take a picture of the backs in full uniform mounted on four horses. Rockne thought that none of them had probably ever been on a horse before, but he agreed to do it.

Rockne was in demand nationally as a football coach. Other universities, including Columbia and Ohio State, made lucrative offers to entice him to leave Notre Dame. However, he had no interest in leaving. He became a syndicated writer and a radio personality and was in demand as an inspirational speaker, particularly for sales meetings for the automotive industry. For the Studebaker Corporation, Rockne developed sales programs based on concepts learned in football but applied to business, as described by Francis Wallace in *Knute Rockne:*

- Selection—ability to select superior human material
- Training—ability to teach his men
- Supervision—salesmen would respond to Rockne's type of discipline
- Inspiration—his understanding contact with individuals as well as the group

On the morning of March 31, 1931, Rockne boarded a Fokker tri-motor for a Kansas City to Los Angeles flight. He was going to Hollywood to sign a film contract. He had been asked to play a coach in a movie that RKO was making.

En route to Wichita, the Fokker encountered icing conditions and was buffeted by a bad storm. Blown off course, the plane crashed. None of the six passengers or crew survived. One theory advanced for the crash was damage to the propeller of the engine on the right wing. A farmer saw the right wing detach from the fuselage, causing the aircraft to dive straight down from about 650 feet.

Rockne was 43 years old when he died. Over 100,000 people lined the streets of South Bend when Rockne's casket was transported from Union Station to Sacred Heart Church on the Notre Dame campus for the funeral Mass. It was attended by 1,400 mourners. The nation was stunned. Mrs. Rockne received many condolences, including messages from President Hoover, ex-President Coolidge, and King Haakon of Norway. Will Rogers, as noted by Francis Wallace in *Knute Rockne,* observed:

> We thought it would take a President or a great public man's death to make the whole nation, regardless of age, race, or creed, shake their heads in real sorrow . . . Well, that's what this country did today, Knute, for you. You died one of our national heroes. Notre Dame was your address but every gridiron in America was your home.

A staff writer for the *Youngstown Vindicator* summarized the nation's feelings about Rockne:

> Anyone who can fire the manhood of others as he did is in every way admirable . . . We all have latent powers that need to be stirred and wakened; Rockne did this, not merely for the men of the Notre Dame squad but for all the healthy young men of the country. Just as we learn history best through the biographies of great men, so in the chronicle of our own time, the life of Knute Rockne, exerting an extraordinary influence for the good, will be remembered.

WINSTON CHURCHILL—British Prime Minister During World War II

“Never give in, never give in, never, never, never, never,—in nothing, great or small, large or petty—never give in except to convictions of honor and good sense.”

Prime Minister Winston Churchill, in a speech at the Harrow School, October 29, 1941

Winston Churchill displayed the quality of perseverance throughout his lifetime with one notable exception, the academic arena. He wasn’t a good student because he didn’t apply himself. His parents decided that he wasn’t suited for the academic rigors of Cambridge or Oxford. Since he had always displayed an interest in the military, they suggested the Royal Military College at Sandhurst, the West Point of Great Britain.

Churchill failed to gain admission to Sandhurst on his first two attempts, but was successful on his third try after taking a cram course taught by a professional tutor. He received no parental praise on his ultimate admission to Sandhurst. His father, Randolph Churchill, wrote: “I am rather surprised at your tone of exultation over your inclusion in the Sandhurst list. There are two ways of winning an examination, one credible, one the reverse. You have unfortunately chosen the latter method and appear too much pleased with your success. Thus the grand result that you came up among the second and third rate class who are only good for commissions in a cavalry regiment.” The top of the class went to the best infantry regiments.

In 1899, Churchill became a celebrity during the Boer War. Retaining his commission in the British army, he went to South Africa as a correspondent for the *Morning Post*. Captured by the Boers when they derailed the train on which he was a passenger, he was escorted to prison in Pretoria. He made plans to escape from prison with two other officers. At the last minute, the two other officers backed down, but Churchill escaped alone to Portuguese East Africa and freedom. He was an instant hero when he arrived back in British-held territory in Durban.

Churchill had lost his first bid for Parliament in the constituency of Oldham prior to leaving for South Africa; however, the publicity surrounding his escape from the Boers helped him to win a seat on his second attempt. He became a vocal and visible Member of Parliament and, in 1908, became president of the Board of Trade.

Churchill advanced through increasingly responsible positions in government. In 1910, he was appointed Home Secretary, a major cabinet post, and, in 1911, when the expansion of the German military became obvious, he was appointed First Lord of the Admiralty. His first major setback was the failure of the Dardanelles campaign, a serious British defeat in World War I, of which he had been the principal architect. He received most of the blame, and he resigned from the Admiralty in 1915 at the age of 41.

Five months later, Churchill was dismissed from the cabinet, although he continued to be a Member of Parliament. He revealed his feelings to a friend: "I'm finished. I am banished from the scene of action." His father had a similar experience at the age of 37 and was never able to overcome it. Not so with Winston who, in his early years in Parliament, was called "Pushful, the younger."

Churchill served creditably with the Sixth Royal Scots Fusiliers in France, until, in 1917, he was asked to become the Minister of Munitions. In 1921, he became the Secretary of State for the Colonies. Earlier, he had left the Conservative Party for the Liberal Party. His party lost favor in 1923, and he left office at the time. He lost his next two campaigns for Parliament.

Churchill approached the Conservative Party about rejoining it and ran as a Conservative candidate. He lost again. Finally, a safe seat was found for him as the candidate from Epping, and he was back in Parliament. Not only was he back in Parliament, but he was appointed to the office of Chancellor of the Exchequer, the second most powerful position in the British government. His father had held the office at the peak of his career. In 1929, however, when the Conservatives were turned out of office, began a 10-year period during which Churchill held no office. At the age of 55, it appeared that his political career was over.

With the increasing threat of war in 1939, Churchill was invited back into the government at his old post of First Lord of the Admiralty. The message, "Winston is back," was sent to all Royal Navy ships and stations. In May 1940, Prime Minister Chamberlain resigned, and Churchill was asked to become Prime Minister. He said that he had nothing to offer the British people but "blood, toil, tears, and sweat."

Summarizing the aim of the British government, Churchill said, "You ask, what is our aim? I can answer in one word: victory—victory at all costs, victory in spite of all terror, victory however long and hard the road may be; for without victory, there is no survival." He played a significant role in the British policy in World War II. "You ask, what is our policy? I will say: It is to wage war by sea, by land, and air, with all our might and all the strength God can give us: to wage war against a monstrous tyranny, never surpassed in the dark, lamentable catalogue of human crime. That is our policy."

Churchill was 65 years old and assuming leadership of a country at war at a time when many of his peers were retiring. However, he felt as if "I were walking with destiny, and that all of my past life has been but a preparation for this hour and this trial."

Churchill was widely recognized as the one to lead Britain during World War II. He said, "Let us therefore brace ourselves to our duties, and so bear ourselves that, if the British Empire and Commonwealth last for a thousand years, men will say, 'That was their finest hour.'" He downplayed his role as leader, according to Mollie Keller in *Winston Churchill:*

> I have never accepted what people have kindly said—namely, that I inspired the nation. Their will was resolute and remorseless, and it proved unconquerable. If it fell to me to express it, and I found the right words you must remember that I have always earned my living by my pen and by my tongue. It was the nation and the race dwelling all around the globe that had the lion's heart. I had the luck to be called upon to give the roar.

* * *

Rockne is a classic example of a promoter of teamwork and of winning. He was willing to be deceptive if it helped to win. Churchill is another case of a man for his time. He believed that all of his life prior to becoming Prime Minister prepared him for leadership, for working with government and military teams, and for winning.

PART II

FAILURE VS. SUCCESS—ROLE MODELS

"Success is not a quantum leap. It is an accumulation of small changes resulting from perseverance, self-discipline, and learning to get the most from your Emotional Intelligence. . . . The question of why some people have become successful, while others struggle throughout their lives and achieve little, has always fascinated mankind. During most of the twentieth century, we were led to believe that it was our cognitive intelligence, our IQ, that determined how well we would do in life. Yet, our common sense and simple power of observation tells us that this simply cannot be the case—that there must be more to success than how well we do in exams in school."

Harvey Deutschendorf, *The Other Kind of Smart*

Part II provides five sets of role models from history that illustrate failure vs. success. A description of the environments within which they strived and the factors that contributed to their success or failure (or limited success) are provided. Because these role models are all inventors / entrepreneurs, other human qualities in addition to Emotional Intelligence traits are discussed, such as fund raising and financial ability, organizational ability, and marketing / product promotion in order to more fully illustrate the environment in which they lived and worked.

Some of the Emotional Intelligence traits demonstrated by these role models include perseverance, optimism, persuasion / negotiation, leadership, motivation, assertiveness, relationships, and teamwork. Other qualities, such as determination and resilience, are also illustrated by their lives.

None of the individuals in Part II who did not accomplish their original goals should be considered complete failures. Financial success is not the only measure of success. Two of these role models considered their development work a contribution so that someone else could finish the work they had started. Ability to communicate and work with others as well as strengths in promoting their efforts were factors in all of the successes. Another two of these individuals, whom some would consider failures, are outstanding examples of perseverance.

CHAPTER 12

INVENTION OF THE STEAMBOAT

ROLE MODELS

John Fitch (1743-1798)

Robert Fulton (1765-1815)

Failure vs. Success

"Genius is only the power of making continuous efforts. The line between failure and success is so fine that we scarcely know when we pass it; so fine that we are often on the line but don't know it. How many a man has thrown up his hands at a time when a little more effort, a little more patience, would have achieved success. As the tide goes out, so it comes in. In business sometimes, prospects may seem darkest when they are really on the turn. A little more persistence, a little more effort, and what seemed hopeless failure may turn into glorious success. There is no failure except in no longer trying. There is no defeat except from within, no really insurmountable barrier save our own inherent weakness of purpose."

Elbert Hubbard

JOHN FITCH—Steamboat Pioneer

"He did persevere. We cannot begin to relate the obstacles he encountered. A considerable volume would scarcely afford the requisite space. Poor, ragged and forlorn, jeered at, pitied as a madman, discouraged by the great, refused by the rich, he and his few friends kept on, until in 1790, they had a steamboat running on the Delaware, which was the first steamboat constructed that answered the purpose of one. It ran with the tide, eight miles an hour, and six miles an hour against it."

National Cyclopedia of American Biography

On a sunny April Sunday in 1785, John Fitch had the idea that led to the development of the steamboat. While walking home from church, hobbled by rheumatism, he watched a neighbor from a nearby town ride by in a horse-drawn carriage. He thought: "What a noble thing it would be if I could have such a carriage without the expense of keeping a horse." His inspiration was to propel a carriage by steam power.

Fitch soon decided against building a steam-propelled wagon because of the poor quality of the roads. However, his experience as a surveyor along the Ohio River motivated him to think about a steam-powered boat. The atmospheric-type of steam engine, such as the engines designed by Newcomen, had been in use for years, but Fitch wasn't familiar with them. In 1785, only three steam engines were in use in the United States, two in New England and one in New Jersey used to pump water from a mine.

Fitch made a sketch of a steam-powered boat. He would have been surprised to learn that, in England, Watt and Bolt were working on a new double-acting design: power was generated on the upward stroke of the cylinder as well as the downward stroke.

Fitch built a model propelled by flat wooden paddles driven by a loop of chain on a sprocket. He also designed a circular paddle wheel similar to those used later on side-wheelers and stern-wheelers on the Mississippi River. His first technical challenge was to transfer the reciprocal motion of the steam engine to the rotary motion of the propeller. Fitch's greatest challenge, however, was obtaining financing for his project. He hoped that the fledgling U.S. Congress would fund his development. In 1785, Fitch petitioned

Congress for financial support of his development effort. Congress referred his petition to a committee who set it aside and ignored it. Unfortunately, it was not entered into congressional records.

Fitch presented his design to Benjamin Franklin, who usually supported the inventions of others. Fitch also presented his proposal, accompanied by his model, drawings, and a written description of the steamboat, to the American Philosophical Society, of which Franklin was the most prominent member. He received no response from either Franklin or the Society.

Later, Fitch learned that Franklin had his own design for powering a boat. Also, James Rumsey of Virginia developed a design for a boat powered by a wheel driven by river current and assisted by men using a system of poles to generate forward motion. Fitch was relieved to hear that the boat wasn't powered by a steam engine. The boat was impractical because it could only travel with the current and because the weight of the men using the poles limited the amount of cargo it could carry.

Fitch also appealed to the State Assemblies in Delaware, Maryland, New Jersey, New York, Pennsylvania, and Virginia for financial support for his venture. He was unable to obtain financial assistance from the States, but they were willing to grant him the exclusive right to operate a steamboat on their rivers; granting that right didn't cost them anything. In March 1786, the New Jersey Legislature granted him exclusive rights for a period of 14 years. In early 1787, Delaware, New York, and Pennsylvania granted him similar rights to those he had obtained from New Jersey.

Unfortunately, venture capitalists didn't exist in the eighteenth century. Fitch organized a joint-stock company with 15 middle-income backers, who included merchants, shopkeepers, and tavern keepers. He sold 20 shares and kept 20 shares for himself.

Fitch chose Henry Voight, a Philadelphia clockmaker and watchmaker, to build a steam engine for his boat. Fitch considered Voight a mechanical genius and, furthermore, a friend at a time when Fitch had few friends. Their first design was a double-acting engine in which power was generated on both the upward and downward strokes. Unfortunately, the size of the cylinder, one inch in diameter, was too small to generate sufficient power to propel the boat. The first trial on a small skiff with flimsy paddles was unsuccessful. Many spectators on the wharf jeered at their efforts.

Fitch's and Voight's next engine had a three-inch-diameter cylinder without a separate condenser. A pump injected water directly into the cylinder, which cooled the steam and produced condensation. This engine wasn't sufficiently powerful to propel the 45-foot skiff in which it was mounted.

The idea for applying power to the paddles came to Fitch in the middle of the night. His "cranks and paddles" idea was implemented by attaching paddles to arms that were moved by a crank. When the crank went downward, paddles were pulled through the water to the stern of the boat; when the crank moved upward, the paddles were lifted out of the water and returned to the bow. This design was used with a steam engine that had a 12-inch-diameter piston.

Fitch and Voight continued to innovate and to improve their design, including the use of a narrower hull with less water resistance. They redesigned the condenser and placed the furnace directly under the boiler, which eliminated the need for bricks and mortar surrounding the furnace.

Voight lost patience with the project, particularly with the shortage of funds. Voight was replaced by William Thornton. Thornton's first design was a condenser used on an engine with an 18-inch-diameter cylinder. The new condenser worked no better than the old one.

Fitch's stockholders, unhappy with his lack of progress, attempted to push him aside and replace him with Thornton. Fitch not only fought off this maneuver, but he designed a straight-tube condenser that worked better than any of Thornton's designs. Fitch and Thornton conducted a series of successful trials using the engine with the larger cylinder and the new condenser.

The Governor of Pennsylvania, Thomas Mifflin, and members of the Pennsylvania Assembly were impressed with the trial run. Fitch scheduled regular, round-trip passenger runs from Philadelphia along the Delaware River to Burlington, Bristol, Bordentown, and Trenton. Fares were kept low to compete with the stagecoach route along the river. In fact, fares were so low that money was lost on every run.

This steamboat's record was otherwise impressive. She carried passengers a total of just under 3,000 miles from mid-May until the end of September 1790 and traveled over 90 miles in 12 1/2 hours, or over seven miles an hour, upstream. Fitch continued to improve his design. He began construction of a second boat that he named, appropriately, *Perseverance*. In mid-October, *Perseverance* broke loose from her moorings, drifted into the Delaware River, and went aground. By the time she was towed back to the wharf, the season was almost over. Personally, Fitch was in dire circumstances. His clothes were in tatters, and, unable to pay his landlady for his room or his meals, he was totally dependent on her charity.

In the spring of 1791, the Commissioners for the Promotion of Useful Arts (Thomas Jefferson, Henry Knox, and Edmund Randolph) settled the Fitch-Rumsey invention dispute by awarding patents to both of them. Fitch was enraged to hear that the design for which he was awarded the patent wasn't his own successful design, but the Bernoulli-Franklin design that Rumsey sponsored. By this stroke, the commissioners gave any possible commercial value of Fitch's invention to Rumsey. Fitch had no recourse because Congress had made no record of his petition to them; the Patent Office wasn't established until 1802.

Fitch lost the support of his financial backers. He wanted to make improvements to *Perseverance*, but he didn't have the money to make them. He tried, unsuccessfully, to obtain additional funding for steamboat development in England and France. On Fitch's last trial on *Perseverance*, Voight arrived at the dock to taunt the inventor dressed in rags and struggling with a sluggish piston. Voight knew how to fix it; furthermore, he knew how to improve it with little expense, but he wasn't going to help his old friend. Fitch's last memory of his steamboat development was this cruel treatment by Voight.

Despite his many disappointments, Fitch said, "I thank God for the perseverance He has given me, in carrying to such length as I have . . . It would have given me heartfelt pleasure could I have rendered more an immediate service than I have, yet please myself with the idea that . . . my feeble attempts will be found of that use which I now wish them to be."

Fitch was technologically successful in his steamboat development, even if his efforts weren't economically successful. In spite of overwhelming setbacks, he proved that a boat could be propelled by steam power.

ROBERT FULTON—Developer of Profitable Steamboats

"As the component parts of all new machines may be said to be old . . . the mechanic should sit down among levers, screws, wedges, wheels, etc. like a poet among the letters of the alphabet, considering them as the exhibition of his thought; in which a new arrangement transmits a new idea to the world." Robert Fulton, quoted in

Cynthia Owen Philip, *Robert Fulton*

Robert Fulton spent the early years of his life in Lancaster, Pennsylvania. In 1780, young Fulton moved to Philadelphia to paint miniature portraits. In 1787, he went to England to study painting with Benjamin West.

Fulton earned enough from the sale of his paintings to support himself, but not enough to pay for work on his inventions. He had a talent for borrowing money to finance his development work. Because he projected an air of trustworthiness, he was able to obtain loans for risky ventures that weren't well-defined.

Development of a submarine became the principal outlet for Fulton's drive. He persuaded the French government to provide development funds. They strung him along because they didn't want to miss an opportunity to overcome their disadvantage with respect to the British navy. When his tests weren't successful, the French government lost interest. Fulton then attempted to interest the British navy in his undersea craft. In 1800, he negotiated with a British agent to move his development work to England. Again, his trials weren't successful. Subsequent trials also failed.

Chancellor Robert Livingston became the principal backer for Fulton's steamboat development. Robert R. Livingston, a wealthy patrician of the Hudson River Valley who had been Chancellor of New York State from 1777 to 1801, arrived in France as the American Minister in 1801. As Chancellor of New York State, Livingston had administered the oath of office to President Washington on April 30, 1789.

Livingston wasn't interested in underwater craft, but he indicated a strong interest in steamboat development. In 1798, the Chancellor acquired John Fitch's New York State rights to steamboat navigation.

While in France, Livingston decided to back Fulton in building a trial vessel. If the trial succeeded, Fulton was to proceed to New York to build a boat that could carry 60 passengers at eight miles per hour from Manhattan to Albany.

The trial in France was moderately successful, and Fulton returned to New York on December 13, 1806. He had moved to England as a young, unsophisticated painter to study painting. He returned as a polished 41-year-old entrepreneur who "looked like a English nobleman." He had negotiated with senior government ministers in both England and France and was endowed with elegance and social graces gained from moving in fashionable society. He was intelligent, refined, and talented, but he wasn't arrogant. Most people who knew him well liked him.

Livingston was granted an extension on his State monopoly until 1823. The monopoly, originally granted in 1803, was contingent on having the first steamboat in operation by April 1807. Fulton installed a Bolton & Watt engine in a 150-foot-long boat with a 13-foot beam and used paddles instead of propellers.

The boat was called *The North River Steamboat of Clermont*. The lower Hudson was called the North River; Clermont was the name of Livingston's estate 110 miles upriver from New York. Initially, the boat was referred to as *The Steamboat*, but eventually she was called *Clermont*.

On August 9, 1807, a secret test run was made on the Hudson River, four years after Fulton's test with his earlier boat on the Seine River in France. The boat achieved a speed of four miles per hour upstream, despite the fact that the paddles were still not completed. The first publicized run was on August 17, 1807. The *Clermont* traveled from Manhattan to Livingston's estate in 24 hours at an average speed of just under five miles an hour; the same average speed was maintained in the last 40 miles to Albany.

On September 4, the first commercial run was made with 14 paying passengers. The *Clermont* accommodated 24 passengers.

In 1808, New York, with a population of 83,000, surpassed Philadelphia as the most populous city in the country. When the Erie Canal was completed in 1825, New York became the undisputed commercial center of the United States. Fulton built 21 steamboats to serve the early years of this market; each one incorporated improvements over the previous model.

Although Fulton is frequently called the inventor of the steamboat, he was really the technologist who built the first commercially successful steam-powered vessel. He built and tested models before proceeding with a full-scale project, and he kept detailed records. He didn't invent any of the components of the steamboat; they had all been invented previously. Rather, he combined components that had previously been determined to be successful and made them into a practical, working unit. He had no formal engineering training, but he brought to the task of building a steamboat years of development on submarines and other technical projects.

Increasing numbers of Fulton steamboats were built for the New York-to-Albany run in the second decade of the 1800s. It was a popular trip because the Hudson has high, rocky banks, and most of the north / south roads were distant from the population centers along the river, such as West Point, Beacon, Newburgh, Poughkeepsie, and Kingston. Providing direct access to these and other river towns was economically feasible.

Fulton used various methods of selling shares in his ventures: advertisements, articles in magazines, lectures, pamphlets, and personal contacts. According to the standards of the time, he was a successful marketer. He selected his employees carefully, trained them well, and gave them wage increases to keep them at work on his projects. His real strengths were in combining quality components into a quality system and in selling that system to the public.

When Livingston died in 1813, his New York monopoly on steamboats was no longer a strong defense against competition. Increasingly, Fulton had to rely on his patents, which weren't strong either. The U.S. Superintendent of Patents from 1802, when the office was established, until 1828 was William Thornton—the same Thornton who had been John Fitch's associate in steamboat development. Thornton considered Fulton's patents worthless.

Thornton observed on the development of the steamboat: "Finding that Robert Fulton, whose genius and talents I highly respect, has been considered by some to be the inventor of the steamboat, I think it is a duty to the memory of John Fitch . . . to show moreover, that if Mr. Fulton has any claim whatever to originality in his steamboat, it must be exceedingly limited."

In January 1815, Fulton, who had a cold, accompanied his lawyer to a hearing in a poorly heated hall in New Jersey. His lawyer was working to repeal the New Jersey law that gave a steamboat monopoly to Fulton's competitor. Fulton was his lawyer's chief witness.

The ferry was delayed by bad weather, causing them to wait in the cold for three hours on the New Jersey side of the river. The lawyer fell through the ice into the river while hurrying to the ferry, and Fulton saved his life. However, the exposure and overexertion made Fulton ill. Three days later, he insisted on inspecting one of his boatbuilding projects. On February 24, 1815, Fulton died of pneumonia.

* * *

A comparison of the personal characteristics of John Fitch and Robert Fulton reveals dramatic differences. Fitch, the pure inventor, was a driven introvert who was perseverance personified. He was willing to endure poverty and depend on the charity of his landlady for room and board. He suffered from ridicule from spectators and criticism from partners who turned against him.

However, Fitch persevered. He was a highly motivated individual who didn't fit the mold of Abraham Maslow's hierarchy of needs. Self-actualization and achievement needs are usually addressed after lower-level needs are fulfilled. Fitch's development work on the steamboat falls into the category of self-actualization and / or achievement needs. He placed satisfying these needs ahead of fulfilling physiological needs such as the need for food, drink, clothing, and shelter.

By comparison, Robert Fulton was a polished, outgoing individual with important social contacts to help finance and promote his development effort. He was more entrepreneur than inventor; his strength was the modification and packaging of things invented by others. Fulton was well-liked; he moved in influential circles.

Fulton was clearly a better fund raiser than Fitch. Fitch spent considerable time and effort obtaining letters of recommendation for use in acquiring financial grants from State governments and from the U.S. Government. Merchants, shopkeepers, and tavern keepers were the shareholders in his joint-stock company. Fitch conducted his development on a shoestring and attempted to support himself.

Fulton moved in higher circles than Fitch and had access to people who could afford to sponsor him. He was successful in his fund-raising efforts, beginning with his early years in England. He was very willing to be supported by sponsors. His path was eased by the financial backing of Chancellor Livingston.

Fulton was considerably more effective than Fitch in the areas of marketing and promotion. Fitch spent all of his time looking inward toward the invention, which is typical for an inventor. Fulton spent time and effort on design and construction tasks, but he continued to promote the steamboat. His work was on a larger scale than Fitch's, and he couldn't tolerate gaps in the flow of financing for his effort.

Fulton is also the winner in a comparison of organizational ability. Fitch had difficulty keeping the services of one key assistant. However, much of this difficulty was due to his financial troubles. Fulton was a strong organizer who managed a much larger and more complex organization than Fitch. Fitch failed and Fulton succeeded, in part, due to factors such as financial acumen, marketing / promotion skills, and organizational ability.

If John Fitch's *Perseverance* had raced Robert Fulton's *Clermont* on the Hudson River in 1807, the *Perseverance* would have arrived at Albany 12 hours before the *Clermont*. However, Fitch carried passengers for only one season with no profits, and Fulton was economically successful in operating multiple passenger boats for a number of years.

CHAPTER 13

INVENTION OF THE TELEPHONE

ROLE MODELS

Philipp Reis (1834-1874)

Alexander Graham Bell (1847-1922)

Failure vs. Success

"If you wish success in life, make perseverance your bosom friend, experience your wise counselor, caution your older brother, and hope your guardian angel."

Joseph Addison

PHILIPP REIS—An Inventor of the Telephone

"Did you ever hear of a man who had striven all his life faithfully and singly toward an object and in no measure obtained it? If a man constantly aspires, is he not elevated?"

Henry David Thoreau

In 1849, at the age of 15, Philipp Reis enrolled in Hassel's Institute at Frankfort-am-Main, Germany, where he developed a serious interest in mathematics and the natural sciences. In 1851, Reis joined the Physical Society of Frankfort and attended their lectures in chemistry and physics and their weekly presentations on new discoveries and inventions in astronomy, physical science, and other scientific subjects.

Reis chose a teaching career and spent the academic year of 1854-55 preparing to become a teacher. He took education courses, worked in a laboratory, and attended lectures in mathematics and science. However, in the spring of 1858, he was offered a position at the Garnier Institute in Friedrichsdorf, Germany. He accepted the offer because of an "ardent desire to make myself right quickly useful" and began teaching in the fall of 1858.

In 1858-59, Reis began his first scientific experiments without the guidance of a mentor. His experiments led to his invention of the telephone in 1860. In his words, according to Sylvanus P. Thompson in *Philipp Reis: Inventor of the Telephone:*

> Incited thereto by my lessons in physics in the year 1860, I attacked a work begun much earlier concerning the organs of hearing, and soon had the joy to see my pains awarded with success, since I succeeded in inventing an apparatus, by which it is possible to make clear and evident the functions of the organs of hearing, but with which also one can reproduce tones of all kinds at any desired distance by means of the galvanic current. I named the instrument "Telephon." The recognition of me on many sides, which has taken place in consequence of this invention, especially the Naturalists' Association . . . at Giessen, has continually helped

> me to quicken my ardor for study, that I may show myself worthy of the luck that has befallen me.

Reis made his first telephones in a small workshop behind his home. He ran wires for his experiments from the workshop to an upstairs room in his house and from the main building of the Garnier Institute to a classroom located across the playground from the main building. His experiments were the first to reproduce sounds at a distance using electromagnetism.

Reis invented "a" telephone; the question is whether or not he invented "the" telephone. The word "telephone" is derived from the Greek words for "far" and "voice." A German writer, Huth, first used the word in 1796 to refer to a megaphone. Sir Charles Wheatstone, the English physicist and telegraph pioneer, used the word in 1840 with its present meaning.

A principal difference between the Reis design and the later design of Alexander Graham Bell is that Reis used an intermittent, direct current provided by a battery, and Bell used an uninterrupted, "undulating" current. In Reis's device, the interrupted current didn't vary in strength with the volume of the sound activating the transmitter as the undulating current did in Bell's design.

Reis's design couldn't reproduce the degrees of loudness and the variations in amplitude and frequency that are the components of sound, both of music and of speech. Vowels were difficult to understand because the device couldn't transmit the amplitude and intensity of the sound—just the pitch and rhythm. It was a more limited device than Bell's, but it worked. Reis demonstrated it on many occasions.

In October 1861, Reis presented his paper "On Telephony by the Galvanic Current" to the Physical Society of Frankfort-am-Main. In November 1861, Reis presented another paper to the Society: "Explanation of a New Theory Concerning the Perception of Chords and of Timbre as a Continuation and Supplement of the Report on the Telephone." In May 1862, Reis lectured and demonstrated his telephone to the Free German Institute at Frankfort.

In 1862, Reis forwarded his paper "On Telephony by the Galvanic Current" to the Annalen der Physik. The society rejected his paper. Reis thought it was because he was "only a poor schoolmaster." However, his paper was forwarded to the Austro-German

Telegraph Society and published in their journal.

In July 1863, Reis demonstrated his telephone to the Physical Society of Frankfort-am-Main. It was also shown to the Emperor of Austria and the King of Bavaria when they visited Frankfort. In February 1864, he exhibited the telephone at a meeting of the Oberhessische Gesellschaft fur Natur und Heilkunde at Giessen. In September 1864, he demonstrated the operation of his telephone to Germany's most distinguished scientists at Giessen at a meeting of the Deutscher Naturforscher and explained its development.

The Physical Society lost interest in his invention, and Reis resigned his membership in the society. The Free German Institute in Frankfort elected him an honorary member and then dismissed his invention as a philosophic toy. His welcome by the scientists at Giessen came too late; he was already ill with tuberculosis that would take his life. By 1872, hemorrhaging of the lungs and an almost total loss of voice prevented him from either teaching or experimenting. In 1873, he gave all of his instruments and tools to the Garnier Institute.

Reis's invention didn't receive the promotion and marketing that usually accompany successful products. He considered himself ahead of his time, so he didn't apply for a patent on his invention. Reis confided to Garnier that he "showed the world the way to a great invention, which must now be left for others to develop." Reis died on January 14, 1874. In 1878, the Physical Society of Frankfort erected a monument to him in the Friedrichsdorf Cemetery. The words "Inventor of the Telephone" are inscribed on the monument.

In 1875, Thomas Edison read the 1860 Reis paper "On Telephony by the Galvanic Current" and conducted his own telephone experiments using a diaphragm and electromagnetism to transmit sound. During the winter of 1876-77, Edison searched for materials whose resistance varied with pressure. He found that carbon was such a material, and he fastened a molded button made of lampblack to a diaphragm for use in a transmitter. In February 1878, he applied for a patent for this transmitter.

Amos Dolbear, who began his experiments with the telephone in August 1876, also benefited from the work of Reis. His transmitter was based on the Reis design. Dolbear considered Reis the real inventor of the telephone. In Silvanus Thompson's biography,

Philipp Reis: Inventor of the Telephone, Dolbear defended Reis's claim:

> Professor Dolbear, the inventor of the "static receiver" form of telephone, is still more explicit in avowing Reis's claim. In the report of his paper on "The Telephone," read March 1882, before the Society of Telegraph Engineers and of Electricians we find: "The speaker could testify that the instrument would talk, and would talk well. The identical instruments employed by Reis would do that, so that Reis's transmitter would transmit. Secondly, his receivers would receive; and Reis did transmit and receive articulate speech with such instruments." As far as Professor Dolbear is concerned, therefore, he admits in unequivocal terms the whole claim of Reis to be the inventor of the telephone.

Even after his death, Reis continued to be a significant influence in the development of telephone technology. Regardless of whether or not he deserves to be called "the" inventor of the telephone, his contribution to its development was crucial. Reis expressed his viewpoint in his autobiographical notes: "As I look back upon my life I can indeed say . . . that it has been 'labour and sorrow.' But I have also to thank the Lord that He has given me a blessing in my calling and in my family, and has been known to bestow more good on me than than I have known to ask of Him."

ALEXANDER GRAHAM BELL—Inventor of the Telephone

"Don't keep forever on the public road, going only where others have gone, and following one after the other like a flock of sheep. Leave the beaten track occasionally and dive into the woods. Every time you do so you will be certain to find something that you have never seen before. Of course it will be a little thing, but do not ignore it. Follow it up, explore all around it; one discovery will lead to another, and before you know it you will have something worth thinking about to occupy your mind. All really big discoveries are the results of thought." Alexander Graham Bell, quoted in

Roger Burlingame, *Out of Silence into Sound*

Alexander Graham Bell's father, Alexander Melville Bell, extended the work of his father by developing "visible speech" and by studying the "anatomy of speech." He studied the use of the lips and tongue in speaking and singing as well as the contribution of breathing and the roof of the mouth to the formation of sounds. He made drawings of the mouth to illustrate how sounds were made in English and other languages. His work was highly regarded; he was a popular teacher of elocution and a university lecturer. His book, *Bell's Standard Elocutionist*, was a best seller.

Alexander Graham Bell grew up surrounded by the studies of his father and grandfather and was profoundly influenced by them. He loved music and studied the piano in his early teens. Young Bell taught elocution and music at a boys' school prior to enrolling at the University of Edinburgh. His work with deaf students was rewarding; while still a young man, he decided to spend his life teaching the deaf to speak.

In August 1870, the Bell family moved to Brantford, Ontario. The principal of the Boston School for the Deaf heard that Alexander Melville Bell had immigrated to Canada and invited him to teach his visible speech concepts to her instructors. He declined because he had accepted a position with a Canadian university; however, he informed the principal that his son was trained in his concepts and would like to come to Boston in his place. Bell started his assignment at the Boston School in April 1871 at the age of 23.

Bell was successful from the beginning, not only because of his knowledge of visible speech, but also because of his patience and deep concern for the children. In addition to his assignment at the Boston School, Bell was professor of vocal physiology in the School of Oratory at Boston University and director of his own School of Vocal Physiology and Mechanics of Speech.

Fortunately, Bell had boundless energy and was able to do several tasks in parallel; also, he didn't require much sleep. When he wasn't teaching, Bell experimented with electrical equipment. Electricity was a popular topic in the 1870s, and the young teacher educated himself in the subject.

Bell was fortunate to have the services of a bright, young technician, Thomas Watson, to make equipment for him. Watson worked in Boston at the shop of Charles Williams, who made experimental equipment for both tinkerers and serious inventors. Williams's speciality was electricity. Bell was given a workbench in Williams's shop. Bell was trying to develop a harmonic telegraph device to send multiple messages simultaneously over a wire.

Bell adapted the device to use an undulatory or wave current, instead of an interrupted direct current. He intended to use an "induced" current, as described by scientists Michael Faraday and Joseph Henry—one that would be alternately a strong and a weak current.

Bell told Watson that "If I can get a mechanism which will make a current of electricity vary in intensity, as the air varies in density when a sound is passing through it, I can telegraph any sound, even the sound of speech." Bell provided Watson with diagrams of the apparatus he had in mind. Bell and Watson were unable to send and receive multiple messages simultaneously. However, Bell couldn't get this idea out of his head.

Bell's work with deaf students was excellent preparation for his experimentation. He had studied the human ear and realized that air waves striking the eardrum were converted to impulses that the brain interpreted as sound.

Bell returned to Boston to prepare a patent application for a harmonic telegraph that could not only send multiple telegraphic signals on a single line simultaneously but also musical tones. Lawyers assisting him with his patent application suggested that he obtain patents on all of the novel devices he was using in his experiments. The moment of epiphany occurred on the afternoon of June 2, 1875. Bell and Watson were working in two rooms 60 feet apart on the top floor of Williams's shop. Watson was working with the transmitters in one room; Bell was adjusting the receivers in the other room. The garret was hot, and the experiment wasn't going well. Watson's temper was rising, and his enthusiasm was dropping. Bell, as usual, was full of energy. In Watson's words, as cited by Roger Burlingame in *Out of Silence into Sound:*

> One of the transmitter springs I was attending to stopped vibrating and I plucked it to start it again. It didn't start and I kept plucking it, when suddenly I heard a shout from Bell in the next room, and then he came out with a rush, demanding "What did you do then? Don't change anything. Let me see!" I showed him. It was very simple.
>
> The contact screw was screwed down so far that it made permanent contact with the spring so that when I snapped the spring the circuit had remained unbroken while that strip of magnetized steel by its vibration over the pole of its magnet was generating that marvelous conception of Bell's—a current of electricity that varied in intensity precisely as the air was varying in density within hearing distance of the spring.
>
> That undulatory current had passed through the connecting wire to the distant receiver which, fortunately, was a mechanism that could transform that current back into an extremely faint echo of the sound of the vibrating spring that had generated it, but what was still more fortunate, the right man had that mechanism at his ear during that fleeting moment—the speaking telephone was born at that moment.

The breakthrough was, to an extent, the result of an accident. The contact screw was screwed down so far that it made permanent contact with the spring, allowing the circuit to remain unbroken and an "undulatory" current of varying intensity to move from the transmitter to the receiver. Another year of experimentation was required before they could send the first clear sentence over the wire. On February 14, 1876, Bell filed his application for a patent accompanied by a diagram of his device; the patent was granted on March 7, 1876.

On March 10, Bell was setting up the equipment for an experiment when he spilled some of the weak sulphuric acid on his clothes. He knew that even though it was diluted, it could burn a hole in his clothing if it wasn't washed off quickly. He summoned Watson to help, saying, "Mr. Watson, come here, I want to see you." Watson heard him in the next room on the receiver. The first complete sentence transmitted over a telephone line wasn't as memorable as Samuel Morse's first message on the telegraph: "What hath God wrought?" However, Bell's message wasn't contrived; it was an unrehearsed request.

Bell conducted one of the first successful one-way distance conversations on the telephone between his parents' home in Brantford, Ontario, and the neighboring town of Mt. Pleasant. The first successful two-way conversation between Boston and Cambridge was followed by a two-way conversation over a 16-mile-long line between Boston and Salem.

On July 9, 1877, Bell and his partners formed the Bell Telephone Company. As the Bell Telephone Company grew, revenue didn't increase fast enough to finance growth. The company offered to sell the Bell patents to the Western Union Telegraph Company. The president of Western Union, answered their offer with a question: "What use would this company make of an electrical toy?"

Later, Western Union answered their own question by convincing Professor Dolbear, owner of a competing design, to assign his telephone patent to their company. Western Union also purchased licenses to Thomas Edison's telephone patents and organized the New England Telephone Company to enter the telephone business. In September 1878, Bell filed suit for infringement, beginning 18 years of litigation; he didn't lose a suit.

Theodore Vail was chosen to guide the expansion of the Bell Telephone Company. He standardized the equipment, implemented policies and procedures for running the organization, and rejected selling the patents. Vail insisted on receiving royalties from the independent telephone companies established around the country.

Litigation in the courts dragged on. Finally, the senior electrical scientist for Western Union suggested buying the Bell patents instead of suing Bell for infringement of patents. The agreement reached by the two companies astounded everyone. Western Union agreed to recognize the Bell patents and retire from the telephone business; Bell bought the Western Union telephone system and agreed to stay out of the telegraph business. Bell bought that subsidiary from Western Union and renamed it Western Electric Company in 1882, the year Bell became a naturalized U.S. citizen.

Bell wasn't a businessman. His principal interests were working with deaf children and inventing. His associate, Thomas Watson, observed, "Bell was a pure scientist. Making money out of his idea never seemed to concern him particularly."

Bell died on August 1, 1922, at the age of 75. All telephone service was suspended for one minute that day in his memory. Bell was buried on the hilltop at Beinn Bhreagh, his summer home in Canada. Inscribed on his headstone are the words "Citizen of the United States and Teacher of the Deaf." No reference to the invention of the telephone was inscribed.

• • •

Philipp Reis and Alexander Graham Bell were pure inventors who weren't interested in the business aspects of financing, marketing, and promoting their invention. Reis was an introvert who worked alone. He had neither a business manager to assist him nor a sponsor. Bell had both.

Reis and Bell were highly motivated individuals. However, Reis was burdened by the lack of recognition for his development efforts. Initially, Reis's work received some attention, but, eventually, the local technical society lost interest. He began to think that his work was premature, that he was ahead of his time, and that others would have to carry his work to its completion.

During the last two years of his life, Reis was too ill to work or to talk. He was 41 when he died. He persevered in his efforts, but he lost his drive toward the end of his life. He wasn't around in the late 1870s when interest in the telephone increased exponentially.

Bell came from a family of achievers. His father and grandfather, experts in speech and hearing, influenced him greatly. Family friends, including one with an expertise in acoustics, provided Bell with built-in consulting support. Bell was a well-liked extrovert. He was the type of individual who could have been a superior marketer and promoter, but those weren't his priorities. His interests were the inventor's interests of developing and improving the product.

Reis's principal shortcoming was his inability to market and promote his ideas on the development of the telephone. He could not convince the scientific community of the value of his invention. Inventors are usually the ones who push their concepts the hardest. Reis was unsuccessful in doing this, even though he demonstrated his device successfully.

Reis's development work was on such a small scale that he did not need large amounts of money to finance it. He financed his work out of his teacher's salary. His family had to live on less to support his work. The highly energetic Bell always had several jobs at one time, and initially he financed his own work. As the demands for development funds increased, Bell was fortunate to have the support of others. Neither Reis nor Bell can be evaluated on their organizational ability. Reis worked alone, and when an individual was needed to manage the Bell Telephone Company, Vail was recruited for the job.

Reis's contributions to the development of the telephone can't be considered a failure. His small-scale effort was one of the key steps along the way in the evolution of the telephone. His contributions would have been even greater had he been a stronger promoter and had he lived longer. He didn't consider himself a failure.

Again, we can ask what the criteria for success are. Financially, Reis wasn't successful in his development work, since he received no income from it. Nevertheless, he contributed to society, and therefore he should be considered somewhat of a success.

Bell was a success by any yardstick by which success is measured. He was financially secure. He received worldwide recognition and many honorary degrees. His work with deaf children ranked him high as a teacher and a humanitarian. Bell's motivation and perseverance were two components of his success. He knew that his idea was a breakthrough, and he wouldn't give up until he had demonstrated that his invention was practicable.

CHAPTER 14

VULCANIZATION DEVELOPMENT

ROLE MODELS

Charles Goodyear (1800-1860)

Thomas Hancock (1786-1865)

Failure vs. Success

"The man who succeeds above his fellows is the one who, early in life, clearly discerns his object, and towards that habitually directs his powers. Even genius itself is but fine observation strengthened by fixity of purpose. Every man who observes vigilantly and resolves steadfastly grows unconsciously into genius."

Edward Bulwer-Lytton

CHARLES GOODYEAR—Developer of Vulcanization

"Charles Goodyear was a man who, having undertaken a thing, could not give it up. He struggled for . . . years—in debt, with a family to support, and exposed to the derision or reproaches of his friends. Several times he was in debtors' prison. He sold his effects, he pawned his trinkets, he borrowed from his acquaintances, he reduced himself and his young family to the severest straits. When he could no longer buy wood to melt his rubber with, his children used to go out to the fields and pick up sticks for the purpose. Always supposing himself to be on the point of succeeding, he thought the quickest way to get his family out of their misery was to stick to India rubber."

National Cyclopedia of American Biography

In 1834, Charles Goodyear inspected an inflatable rubber life preserver in a store operated by the Roxbury India Rubber Company of Roxbury, Massachusetts, and realized that he could improve the design of the life preserver's inflation valve. He described the new valve design to the store manager, who agreed that Goodyear had invented a better valve. However, the manager added that unless the quality of rubber products could be improved, the new valve design had no value because rubber products were returned daily.

Natural rubber products melted and became sticky and odoriferous in warm weather and very brittle and unyielding in cold weather. In Goodyear's opinion: "Rubber is such a wonderful substance. If only a way could be found to keep it from melting in the summer and getting brittle in the winter, it would be useful to mankind in a thousand ways."

Goodyear began working with rubber using his wife's pots, pans, rolling pin, and oven in the kitchen of their rented home; he couldn't afford to rent a shop to use for his experiments. Goodyear attempted to manufacture several hundred pairs of crude rubber shoes. He made them during the winter and stored them to determine what effect the summer heat would have on them. Equipment for controlled temperature experiments didn't exist at that time. He had to wait for the change of season to check his results. The smell of the sticky, melting lumps was obvious to the entire neighborhood.

Goodyear concluded that the process for which he was searching involved adding a substance to the raw rubber, so he experimented with additives. He commented, "I was encouraged in my efforts by the reflection that what is hidden and unknown, and cannot be discovered by scientific research, will most likely be discovered by accident, if at all, and by the man who applies himself most perseveringly to the subject and is the most observing."

To promote rubber products, Goodyear wore clothing made from rubber and carried a hard rubber cane. A person who inquired how to find him was told: "If you see a man in an India-rubber coat, India-rubber shoes, and India-rubber cap, and in his pockets an India-rubber purse with not a cent in it, that is Charles Goodyear."

In 1838, Goodyear reached a turning point when he met Nathaniel Hayward, who had lost his job when a shoe factory closed. Hayward used the empty shoe factory for his rubber experiments. He tried sulfur as an additive and achieved the same results as Goodyear's acid process in drying the rubber and removing the stickiness. Hayward agreed to work as Goodyear's assistant. Goodyear encouraged Hayward to obtain a patent on his sulfur additive process; he bought Hayward's patent rights in 1839.

Goodyear tried unsuccessfully to combine his acid process and Hayward's sulfur process. Goodyear's next break was a U.S. Government contract to make 150 waterproof mailbags. He produced the mailbags, hung them up by the handles, and went away during a summer hot spell. Upon his return, he found the handles stretched and the bags on the floor in a softened, smelly mess. He had received considerable publicity on his government contract; however, he was disappointed again. He concluded that his current process worked well on the surface of his rubber products and on thin rubber, but it failed with thicker rubber.

Goodyear had similar results with other rubber products. His commercial reputation suffered; consumers wouldn't buy his products, and he was penniless again. The Goodyears sold their household possessions one more time. His friends advised him to give up his pursuit of rubber as a usable, practical material. Goodyear had discovered only half of what became known later as the vulcanization process for rubber; he was about to discover the other half.

In January 1839, Goodyear heated mailbag rubber on a wood stove in a house in Woburn, Massachusetts. He shifted the rubber from one hand to the other while talking with his brother and two friends. In gesturing, he accidentally dropped a piece of the rubber on the stove. It hardened like leather instead of melting, as rubber usually did. Goodyear became very excited when he saw the result; he realized that he had discovered a key step in his ultimate process. In his words, as noted by C. J. Hylander in *American Inventors:*

> I carried on at my dwelling place some experiments to ascertain the affect of heat on the compound that had decomposed in the mailbags and other articles. I was surprised that a specimen, being carelessly brought into contact with a hot stove, charred like leather. I directly inferred that if the charring process could be stopped at the right point, it might divest the compound of its stickiness throughout, which would make it better than the native gum.
>
> Upon further trials with high temperatures I was convinced that my inference was sound. When I plunged India rubber into melted sulfur at great heats, it always charred, never melted. What was of supreme importance was that upon the border of the charred fabric there was a line which had escaped charring and was perfectly cured.

Goodyear had made a major breakthrough, but he faced an uphill struggle. He and others had announced product improvements in the past, and the public had been disappointed repeatedly. Consumers weren't willing to buy rubber goods.

Goodyear tried varying the temperature of the rubber. Initially, he used small kitchen stoves for his work, but they were inadequate. Then he used furnaces in nearby factories. The Goodyear family again relied upon friends and neighbors for gifts of food and heating fuel in the winter. He also depended on others to provide the raw materials for his work.

Goodyear and his sons built a crude brick oven so they would not have to beg foremen to use their furnaces at times that were unpredictable. He traded rubber products, such as rubber aprons, for the bricks and mortar, since he had no money.

Goodyear then rented a factory to produce sheet rubber products. Again, he got into financial difficulty and was lent money by his brother-in-law. In 1844, Goodyear applied for a patent in the United States for his 1839 discovery.

Goodyear wanted to apply simultaneously for patents in the United States, England, and France, but he couldn't afford to make all of the samples to apply for the patents. Also, he didn't have the money to travel to England and France to apply; nevertheless, he was awarded a patent in France in 1844, the same year that he was awarded his U.S. patent.

When Goodyear applied for a patent in England, he was told that an English rubber experimenter, Thomas Hancock, had applied for a patent earlier. In his struggle to promote rubber, Goodyear had given away many samples. A sample had been taken to England, where it was examined by Thomas Hancock. It wasn't difficult for him to determine that Goodyear's rubber contained sulfur. In effect, Hancock, who had worked with rubber for years, rediscovered the vulcanization process. Goodyear unsuccessfully contested Hancock's patent in the English courts.

Goodyear could have been a wealthy man if he had been a shrewder businessman. He let money flow through his hands by licensing his process to other manufacturers for a pittance and by spending excessively to display rubber products at expositions and exhibits. However, he was aggressive in protecting his patents against theft, and several of his cases went to the Supreme Court. A well-known case was against a man who used Goodyear's patent without remuneration and claimed to have discovered vulcanization. Daniel Webster took a leave of absence as Secretary of State to defend Goodyear's interests. Webster won "The Great India Rubber Suit" in court after a skillful two-day defense.

Goodyear's exhibit at the "Exhibition of the Works of All Nations" at the Crystal Palace in London was elaborate. He spent $30,000, all of his savings plus borrowed money, on the exhibit, which was centrally located in the main hall and was made entirely of rubber, including sofas, chairs, trays, fans, buttons, canes, combs, and brushes.

In 1854, Goodyear had a more elaborate exhibit at the world's fair in Paris than he had in London. Through a technicality in the French law, his French patent was declared invalid. Nevertheless, he was awarded the Cross of the Legion of Honor by Louis Napoleon.

Charles Goodyear was $200,000 in debt when he died on July 1, 1860. He considered his life a success; he didn't die a bitter man. His life's work generated fortunes for others, and his own lack of financial success didn't bother him. He wrote, "Life should not be estimated exclusively by the standard of dollars and cents. I am not disposed to complain that I have planted and others have gathered the fruits. A man has cause for regret when he sows and *no one* reaps."

Much of Goodyear's recognition came after his death. In 1939, a statue of Charles Goodyear was unveiled in Akron, Ohio, the rubber capital of the United States, to commemorate his discovery on the wood stove in Woburn in 1839. The Goodyear Tire and Rubber Company was named for him, although it was incorporated many years after he died.

Although synthetic rubber derived from petroleum is used today in making tires, a vulcanization process similar to the one discovered by Goodyear is still in use. In 1976, Goodyear was inducted into the National Inventors' Hall of Fame. He was a member of a select group honored for their technological advances generated through the patent system.

THOMAS HANCOCK—Founder of the Rubber Industry in Great Britain

"Life affords no higher pleasure than that of surmounting difficulties, passing from one step of success to another, forming new wishes and seeing them gratified. He that labors in any great and laudable undertaking has his fatigues first supported by hope and afterwards rewarded by joy."

Dr. Johnson

In 1820, Thomas Hancock established the world's first rubber factory in England and founded the modern rubber industry. As a London coach maker, he had used rubber as a waterproofing material in clothing for his coach passengers. He made his first rubber products by dissolving rubber in turpentine; they weren't successful. His next products were made by using rubber as elastic in articles of clothing such as suspenders, garters, gaiters, gloves, stockings, trousers, and waistcoats.

Hancock discovered the importance of heat in treating rubber while making rubber bands for these products. Hancock cut strips of rubber for use as elastic bands from blocks of rubber and from rubber bottles imported from South America. On April 29, 1820, he was granted an English patent for this use of rubber.

From 1820 to 1847, Hancock was awarded 16 English patents for rubber processes and products, several of which involved mixing another component with rubber. He used oil of turpentine in manufacturing sheet rubber, and he discovered that pitch and tar could also be combined with rubber. A mixture of rubber and pitch was used under the copper sheathing of ships' bottoms as protection against worms attacking the wooden hulls.

Charles MacIntosh, inventor of waterproof fabrics, was an early contemporary of Hancock in the rubber business. He overcame the problem of rubber becoming sticky in warm weather by placing it between two fabrics. In 1823, he was granted an English patent for raincoats made this way. MacIntosh called his raincoats "waterproof double textures"; his customers called them "macintoshes."

In 1825, Hancock was licensed to manufacture macintoshes. In 1830, Hancock began to manufacture his rubber products at the MacIntosh plant in Manchester from masticated rubber shipped from his factory in London.

Hancock had an early encounter with sulphur-treated rubber samples in 1842, as he noted in his *Personal Narrative*:

> Some time in the early part of the autumn of 1842, Mr. Brockedon (coiner of the term "vulcanization" based on Vulcan, the god of fire from Roman mythology) showed me some small bits of rubber that he told me had been brought by a person from America, who represented himself as an agent of the inventor [Goodyear]; it was said that they would not stiffen by cold, and were not affected by solvents, heat, or oils. . . .

In late 1842 and early 1843, Hancock conducted experiments treating rubber to prevent its stiffening in cold temperatures. He attempted to produce a "single texture" raincoat with just one layer of fabric and one layer of rubber. He had tried similar experiments 20 years earlier without success.

Goodyear's discovery of the vulcanization process for rubber occurred in early 1839 when he observed the effect of heat applied to rubber in combination with sulphur and lead salts. Goodyear submitted his specification for the process to the U.S. Patent Office in December 1841. Goodyear gave samples of his vulcanized rubber to a young Englishman visiting the United States, and asked him to find a British manufacturer willing to buy the process.

Goodyear wasn't alone in thinking that the secret of the process by which he "changed" rubber couldn't be deduced by studying the samples. The young man showed the samples to Brockedon, an inventor who had contacts with the MacIntosh Company. The young man returned to America without obtaining the agreement from the MacIntosh Company to buy the process.

Unfortunately for Goodyear, he left samples with Brockedon who passed them on to Hancock. Hancock realized the importance of the samples and immediately conducted experiments to duplicate them. It wasn't difficult for him to detect that sulphur had been used in the process. Once Hancock had evidence that the "change" in rubber for which he had been searching for 20 years could be accomplished, he attempted to rediscover the process. He worked alone in his laboratory for more than a year, and "resolved, if possible, not to be outdone by any." He did, however, use the advice of experts, such as chemists.

Hancock was close to duplicating the process when he applied for a provisional patent on November 21, 1843, just weeks before Goodyear applied for a patent in England. Hancock, according to English law, had six months to complete his process, and, on May 30, 1844, he was granted the patent. When Goodyear applied for an English patent, it was denied even though Hancock later admitted under oath that the first vulcanized rubber he had seen was from the United States.

The principles followed by the British patent authorities at this time were different from those followed by the American and German patent offices. The main objective of the British was to register claims to patents, not to guarantee the originality or the validity of the patent. In the United States and Germany, the inventor had to prove that his patent was "novel and deserving." Inequities existed in many of the early patent processes.

Another English technologist, Alexander Parkes, inventor in 1846 of a cold process of vulcanization using a chemical process without heat, wrote in his copy of Hancock's *Personal Narrative,* as cited by William Woodruff in *The Rise of the British Rubber Industry During the Nineteenth Century*:

> I think it is a sad thing for Mr. Thomas Hancock to try to claim the discovery of vulcanization from the fact of the vulcanized rubber first being brought by Goodyear from America and pieces given to Brockedon "Hancock's co-partner" and others. These were seen, examined and experimented on by several and it was found to be free sulphur in a heated and molten state that produced the permanent elasticity of rubber. The above facts were related to me both by Brockedon and Thomas Hancock.

* * *

A comparison of the personal characteristics of Charles Goodyear, the inventor, and Thomas Hancock, the entrepreneur / inventor, is similar to a comparison between steamboat developers John Fitch and Robert Fulton. Goodyear is another example of a driven individual enduring hardships to continue his development activities.

Goodyear was willing to let his family go hungry, wear worn-out clothing, and suffer winter cold due to a lack of heating fuel. At times, his family was totally dependent on relatives and friends. Goodyear tolerated these conditions because he thought if he continued his experiments with rubber, success was just around the corner. In his opinion, the best way to help his family was to find a way to make rubber a useful product.

With respect to perseverance, Fitch and Goodyear were in a class by themselves. They were so dedicated to their development efforts that they never considered giving up. Goodyear is another example of a highly motivated individual who didn't fit the pattern of Abraham Maslow's hierarchy of needs. He addressed his self-actualization and achievement needs first, finding a way to make rubber useful and to market it successfully. Satisfying his physiological needs, such as food, drink, clothing, and shelter, were a lower priority.

Goodyear's English competitor, entrepreneur / inventor Thomas Hancock, was a more practical businessman than Goodyear. Hancock started manufacturing rubber products in England in 1820, 14 years before Goodyear became interested in rubber. Hancock was successful in manufacturing and selling rubber products, even with their early shortcomings.

Goodyear, in contrast with Hancock, not only displayed samples of his vulcanized rubber, but left samples with his competitors. He didn't think that anyone could deduce his process from samples. He was wrong. By 1842, Hancock had 22 years of experience in the rubber industry. When he realized that rubber could be processed to make useful products in forms other than thin sheets and strips, he focused on rediscovering the process. He was aware of the gaps in his knowledge and was willing to consult with expert chemists to fill those gaps. In 1842-43, he concentrated on duplicating the discovery of the vulcanization process.

Assertiveness, a key ingredient of success for entrepreneurs as demonstrated by Hancock, is a desirable quality. Entrepreneurs realize that an improved product or process is only one factor contributing to success, although it is a major one. They must also market and promote the product actively.

Hancock didn't do anything illegal in the pursuit of his vulcanization patent in England. In fact, the London patent office operated in a way that favored English inventors over foreign inventors. Nevertheless, Hancock's refusal to acknowledge Goodyear's contribution to his success was the action of a small man.

Hancock was a stronger financial manager than Goodyear. If Goodyear had made better financial decisions, he would have been a wealthy man. The fees that Goodyear charged for his licenses weren't sufficient to recover his development costs and to finance his manufacturing operations. He had the outlook of an inventor, not a businessmen. Promoting the usefulness of rubber was more important to him than making a profit. Earnings weren't a high priority with him. Goodyear's excessive spending on displays of rubber products is also questionable.

Hancock certainly had more organizational ability than Goodyear. He succeeded where Goodyear failed for several reasons, including Goodyear's lack of financial ability. Hancock beat Goodyear to the English patent for the vulcanization of rubber, but Goodyear could have been financially successful with just his U.S. patent. Goodyear did, however, successfully defend his patents in infringement suits in court.

In terms of profits of the enterprise, Goodyear was a failure, and Hancock was a success. A comparison of Goodyear and Hancock provides us with another example of relative success and success, not necessarily of failure and success.

CHAPTER 15

INVENTION OF THE SEWING MACHINE

ROLE MODELS

Elias Howe (1819-1867)

Isaac Singer (1811-1875)

Failure vs. Success

"Firmness of purpose is one of the most necessary sinews of character, and one of the best instruments of success. Without it, genius wastes its efforts in a maze of inconsistencies."

Philip Dormer Stanhope

ELIAS HOWE—Inventor and Litigant

"I'm proof of the word 'failure.' I've seen behind it. The only failure a man ought to fear is failure in cleaving to the purpose he sees to be best."

George Eliot

One of Elias Howe's early jobs was in Boston with Ari Davis, a maker of marine instruments and scientific equipment. Davis was consulted by many inventors in the area and was known both for his good advice and for his outspokenness. An inventor brought a knitting machine to Davis's shop to obtain advice and was asked why he bothered with knitting machines when he could be doing something worthwhile, such as inventing a sewing machine. Howe overheard the conversation, including Davis's comment about the fortune that would accompany such an invention. Howe tucked the thought away for future reference.

Howe watched his wife sew and became convinced that he could devise a machine that could duplicate her sewing motions. He had the mind of an inventor, and ideas began to flow. A friend and classmate invested in Howe's effort to develop a sewing machine in return for a 50 percent interest in the patent. Inventing the sewing machine was an evolutionary process; many inventors added to or improved upon earlier designs.

Howe spent several months designing and building his first model of a sewing machine. In July 1845, he sewed two wool suits, one for his friend and one for himself, using the machine.

Howe struggled to convince the public of the value of his sewing machine. He arranged a sewing contest at a clothing factory featuring five of their fastest seamstresses vs. his machine. A straight seam was given to each of the five seamstresses, and five straight seams were given to Howe. Not only did he finish first, but his seams were judged to be the straightest and the strongest. Howe's machine could sew 250 stitches a minute, approximately seven times faster than a seamstress. If the contest had involved any seam other than a straight one, his machine couldn't have done it, however.

Winning the contest should have helped to promote sales of his machine, but the mill owners thought that it was too expensive. At that time, a machine cost at least $300 to build. Also, the public thought that sewing machines would put many people out of work. Sales of Howe's machine were disappointing. He constructed a second machine with a few improvements, submitted it to the patent office with his patent request, and was granted a patent on September 10, 1846.

Howe's friend became discouraged when no orders were received, and he refused to provide further financial support. Howe obtained a loan from his father and constructed a third sewing machine that his brother took to England to promote sales there.

The only offer his brother received was from William Thomas, who employed 5,000 workers manufacturing corsets, carpet bags, umbrellas, valises, and leather products. Thomas offered Howe $1,250 for the machine and a weekly wage to adapt it for use in corset manufacturing. On February 5, 1847, Howe sailed for England. Over a period of eight months, Howe redesigned his sewing machine for use in manufacturing corsets.

Thomas made a verbal agreement with Howe to patent the machine in England and to pay him a royalty for each machine that he sold. However, he didn't pay Howe, even though Thomas received £10 (five dollars) on each machine sold in England. By the time that he died, Thomas had earned $1 million on his $1,250 investment. Thomas became overbearing with Howe and assigned him to menial tasks. Howe quit his job with Thomas and found himself unemployed and miles from home.

When Howe returned to New York in April 1849 after spending two years in England, he found that interest in sewing machines had increased considerably. He was surprised to see that many of the machines on the market infringed on his patent. He contacted all of the sewing machine manufacturers, informed them of his patent, and asked them for payment for licenses and royalties.

Some manufacturers were willing to pay for the use of Howe's patent initially, but others who weren't willing talked those who were out of paying Howe what they owed him. Howe had no alternative but to sue.

The main obstacle in the litigation initiated by Howe was Isaac Singer, inventor of an improved sewing machine that worked well. Singer had borrowed many ideas from previous machines, including Howe's machine. He was more aggressive than the other manufacturers and was determined to fight Howe in court. The issue of originality was cloudy because so many individuals had contributed to the present configurations of sewing machines.

In late 1850, Howe went to New York to supervise the manufacture of 14 sewing machines made to his design. Howe's principal source of income was from licensing his patent to other manufacturers, not from profits received from the manufacture of sewing machines. Litigation, not manufacturing, had been his strength so far.

Singer didn't claim to be the inventor of the sewing machine. His main defense in the lawsuit with Howe was that Howe wasn't the inventor either, and that earlier inventors had prior claim to most of Howe's design. However, the early designers had never filed a patent. Singer lost his lawsuit with Howe in 1854.

After the settlement, all manufacturers were required to pay a 25-dollar royalty to Howe for each machine they sold. Nevertheless, all major manufacturers, including Singer and Company, claimed that the others were infringing on their patents. No single inventor, including Howe, could build sewing machines without claims of infringement from the others. In 1856, they were all headed for more litigation in Albany, New York.

It was suggested that a "combination" of sewing machine manufacturers be formed to eliminate the ongoing litigation. All of the major manufacturers formed a patent pool to allow each of them to produce machines with all of the current features.

Initially, Howe objected to the combination, but he joined after his conditions were met: licensing of a minimum of 24 manufacturers, payment of a royalty of five dollars to Howe on each machine sold in the United States, and a royalty of one dollar for each machine sold outside the United States. This agreement made Howe a wealthy man. He earned $2 million in royalties from 1856 to 1867, when the term of his patent expired.

The combination charged a 15-dollar license fee on each machine to all manufacturers, including themselves. The license fee was used to pay for litigation against infringers and to pay Howe his royalty; any remainder was split among the members of the combination. Howe's patent was renewed in 1860, and the license fee was lowered from 15 dollars to seven dollars. At that time, Howe's royalty was reduced to one dollar per machine, which remained in effect until his patent expired in 1867. Most of the commonly-used features of the machine became public property, motivating many additional manufacturers to enter the field.

Howe was a good-looking, outgoing man with considerable personal charm. However, after living in poverty in his early years and enduring the experience of having to fight to protect his patents, he became less outgoing and more quiet and reserved. He was known for his gifts to charity in his later years. He won a gold medal in Paris at the 1867 World's Fair for one of the Howe Machine Company sewing machines and was awarded the Cross of the Legion of Honor by France. On October 3, 1867, he died of pneumonia in Brooklyn, New York.

ISAAC SINGER—Sewing Machine Inventor and Promoter

"People are always blaming their circumstances for what they are. I don't believe in circumstances. The people who get on in this world are the people who get up and look for the circumstances they want, and, if they don't find them, make them."

George Bernard Shaw, *Mrs. Warren's Profession,* Act II

Isaac Singer left home at the age of 12, in his words, "without money, without friends, without education, and possessed of nothing but a strong constitution and a prolific brain" [and without humility]. Singer was good-looking, over six feet tall, blond, and outgoing. He possessed considerable assertiveness and charisma, and he had a knack for winning people over to his viewpoint. Women were charmed by him; he instilled trust in people. He was an amateur actor in his spare time.

Singer worked for a press and developed a machine for carving wooden type for printers. However, Singer's timing was off; wooden type was being replaced by lead type. At this time, Singer was 38 years old, and, by any criteria, couldn't be considered a success. However, his personal qualities of motivation and boundless optimism wouldn't let him settle into a secure but quiet existence. He was a driven man.

George Zieber, a Philadelphia book publisher and jobber, financed the manufacture of a type-carving machine based on Singer's design that was completed in June 1850 and transported to Boston by Singer and Zieber in search of sales. They rented a room on the first floor of Orson Phelps's shop in Boston next door to the main factory area, where Phelps constructed sewing machines designed by J. H. Lerow and S. C. Blodgett.

The Lerow and Blodgett machine used a shuttle that moved in a circular motion instead of back and forth as on other designs. The machine didn't work well and required frequent maintenance. Phelps asked Singer whether he and Zieber could redesign the machine at their own expense and make it more reliable. Singer assured Phelps that he could do the redesign, and that Zieber had money available to finance the development work.

Phelps convinced Singer that more money could be made from

sewing machines than from type-carving machines, which had a very limited market. Singer developed a credo that helped to establish his fortune: "I don't give a damn for the invention, the dimes are what I am after." That statement distinguished Singer, the entrepreneur, from Singer, the inventor. Clearly, Singer was primarily an entrepreneur.

Singer redesigned the Lerow and Blodgett machine. Phelps, Singer, and Zieber signed an agreement in which Phelps and Zieber each put up the money to build a model of the machine to obtain a patent, and Singer contributed his ability as an inventor.

Singer worked 12-hour days and skipped many meals to complete the machine in 11 straight days. He took the machine to New York to begin the patent application process. The application was one of the early steps in revolutionizing the clothing industry, the shoe industry, and many other businesses that involved sewing.

When Singer and Zieber began to market their machine, they encountered considerable resistance from those who had tried earlier sewing machines and been dissatisfied with them. People were also concerned that sewing machines would displace thousands of tailors and seamstresses. Also, the price of the machines was more than shops in the clothing industry could afford to pay. Initially, sewing machines couldn't be sold to housewives for use in the home because of their high price.

Singer was in his element in promoting sales of his sewing machine. The actor in him came out as he demonstrated his sewing machine at carnivals and circuses, in rented halls, and wherever people would listen to his pitch. He wrote articles promoting the machines, advertised heavily, and sent out agents to tout the advantages of the sewing machine. Singer was an actor, an inventor, and an entrepreneur, but he demonstrated strongly in this phase of his life that he was, above all, a promoter.

In late 1850, Singer rented space in a clothing store to demonstrate his sewing machine. Elias Howe saw the demonstration and realized that Singer had infringed upon his patents. Howe approached Singer at the machine shop and offered to sell the rights to his patent for $2,000. Singer argued with him and threatened to kick him down the stairs. Singer was frustrated because he and Zieber couldn't raise that amount, even if they wanted to. It was the best offer they ever received from Howe; in fact, they ultimately paid Howe considerably more for the use of his patent.

Zieber had a liquidity problem. The business was saved when orders were received. Singer planned to use part of the money to buy out Phelps. He picked quarrels with Phelps and treated him in a condescending manner.

Singer promised Phelps $1,000 down and $3,000 additional in three installments, along with a verbal agreement to keep his shop busy for five years, the duration of the partnership. Phelps, who wasn't strong enough to contest Singer's aggressive pitch, signed the contract on December 24, 1850. Singer immediately told Phelps that he would have to go on the road selling machines, which Phelps didn't want to do. Singer then sold Phelps's one-third interest to a businessman and treated him as he had treated Phelps.

Singer realized that neither he nor Zieber had the necessary financial or legal background to deal with the venture as it grew. Singer visited Edward Clark, a partner in the law firm of Jordan, Clark, and Company, who had drawn up the contracts for the partnership. Singer offered Clark a one-third share of the business for his services. Clark was the one partner whom Singer couldn't bully. He seemed to have a hold on Singer. Clark told Zieber that, "Singer will not break the agreement I shall make with him." Clark was a vital addition to the enterprise and the source of many innovations that generated profits for the business.

In December 1851, Zieber became ill, and his doctor confined him to bed. He became concerned that if anything happened to him, the friends from whom he had borrowed wouldn't be paid. Singer offered him $6,000 for his share of the business (annual profits at that time were $25,000). Clark drew up the agreement; Zieber signed it in bed the next morning.

Zieber recovered within a short time and realized his mistake. He had given up all claim to Singer's patents and had been replaced as a 50 percent patent holder by Clark. Singer and Zieber had operated as friends (most of the time) as well as partners. Clark and Singer didn't have the same relationship; they were antagonists from their first meeting.

In 1851, Howe visited the Singer and Clark venture to request $25,000 for a license to use his patent and was thrown out again. Clark underestimated the validity of Howe's claim and made a poor business decision, a rarity for him. As before, the Singer partnership ultimately would pay Howe much more than the amount he had requested. During the next three years, almost all of the partnership's profits and most of Clark's energy were spent on legal battles. By 1853, other major sewing machine manufacturers had signed licenses with Howe to use his patent.

In July 1854, Howe won his suit against Singer and threatened to sue him in New Jersey as well as New York. Singer was directed to pay Howe $15,000 and a royalty of 25 dollars per machine. Litigation among the manufacturers of sewing machines didn't settle down until 1856, when one of the sewing machine manufacturers suggested the "combination," a patent pool in which all companies in the combination had the use of the other company's patents for a fee.

In 1855, the United States was in an economic slump—the worst since 1837. Singer sold only 883 machines and was struggling after making payments to Howe. Also that year, Singer designed a smaller, lighter machine for use in the home. The cost of the machine was $125 at a time when the average annual family income was $500. Clearly, housewives needed help in purchasing their first sewing machine. Clark had the idea of leasing the sewing machine to the housewife and applying the lease payments toward the purchase of the machine. Clark's installment plan idea boosted sales to 2,564 machines in 1856; sales tripled in one year.

Clark also suggested selling sewing machines for half price to church ministers to use in establishing sewing societies associated with their churches to show that respectable women sewed. This also introduced the sewing machine to groups and familiarized individual housewives with it.

The production of sewing machines grew rapidly after 1858. By 1870, Singer had produced 127,833 machines using mass production techniques, such as the use of interchangeable parts—a concept devised by Eli Whitney.

European sales were a principal reason for the rapid growth of I. M. Singer and Company; Singer's competitors didn't exploit foreign markets nearly as aggressively as he did. By 1861, Singer had sold more machines in Europe than in the United States. Singer was one of the earliest multinational corporations.

In 1863, Clark and Singer agreed to dissolve their partnership and form a joint stock company. Each received 40 percent of the stock in the company plus an equal share of the bond holdings, and both men agreed to step down from active management of the company. Neither wanted the other in charge; if Clark wanted Singer to give up his control, he would have to give up control also.

Singer developed a heart condition, and the combination of a chill and heart problems caused his death on July 23, 1875. Isaac Singer's life was certainly a Horatio Alger story. He made significant contributions as an inventor. His drive and aggressiveness contributed significantly to his success. However, his ability to promote the sewing machine, using skills developed as an actor, was his most important accomplishment.

• • •

A comparison of Elias Howe and Isaac Singer is a comparison of two entrepreneur / inventors. Both men were extroverts who possessed creative mechanical ability. With their outgoing nature, they made friends easily. Singer was the more aggressive and strong-willed of the two and was less affected by the setbacks that he encountered. Howe was changed in contending with many obstacles in his path to success. Later in life, he was a more subdued and a less outgoing individual than he had been as a young man.

Howe and Singer were endowed with perseverance and determination. They were highly motivated, and both knew poverty early in their lives. Howe was a businessman as well as an inventor; he didn't indulge in dubious business practices.

In contrast, Singer was self-centered and had questionable business ethics, particularly in his treatment of his partners. He treated them unfairly, but his treatment of his friend and partner, Zieber, was particularly unkind.

Determining whether Howe or Singer was stronger in the financial arena is difficult. In their early development efforts, both were able to obtain minimum financing for their development work. However, Singer realized that he lacked skill in raising money, knowledge of legal matters, and experience in organizational tasks. He brought in Clark to deal with those issues. Once Clark overcame the early patent problems, he contributed heavily to the growth of the venture. Singer knew that he needed Clark, but couldn't control him once he had him.

Singer was, by far, a better marketer and promoter than Howe. As a promoter, Singer had few equals. The ham in him, developed during his many formative years as an actor, created a promoter of the highest order. Howe didn't have to function as a marketer or a promoter until late in life when he began to manufacture sewing machines.

Howe's organizational ability is difficult to evaluate because of his late entry into manufacturing. Singer had a reasonably strong organizational ability, but increasingly left business decisions to Clark, a stronger organizer. In terms of strategic ability, Howe was intelligent enough to comprehend the economic benefits of litigation. Clark made many of the strategic decisions for I. M. Singer & Company, such as instituting the installment plan and the expansion into Europe. Today, most people think of Singer, not Howe, when they think of the sewing machine.

Evaluation of failure vs. success with respect to the sewing machine is not clear cut. Again, Howe was more successful as a litigant; Singer was more successful as a promoter. Singer knew how to choose a business partner; however, Howe knew how to select a patent attorney. Financially, both were successful. As human beings, Howe's gifts to charitable institutions late in life place him ahead of Singer.

However, if success is measured by the accomplishment of the organizations that they left behind, there is no contest. I. M. Singer & Company, later the Singer Company, significantly outdistanced the accomplishments of the Howe Machine Company.

CHAPTER 16

INVENTION OF THE AIRPLANE

ROLE MODELS

Samuel Langley (1834-1906)

The Wright Brothers,
Wilbur (1867-1912) and Orville (1871-1948)

"The real difference between men is energy. A strong will, a settled purpose, an invincible determination, can accomplish almost anything; and in this lies the distinction between great men and little men."

Buckminster Fuller

SAMUEL LANGLEY—Early Aircraft Inventor

"Because a fellow has failed once or twice, or a dozen times, you don't want to set him down as a failure 'til he's dead or loses his courage—and that's the same thing."

George Horace Larimer

In 1887, Samuel Langley was appointed secretary (director) of the Smithsonian Institution. In 1888, he published *The New Astronomy*, which became a classic in the field. Three of his most important contributions at the Smithsonian were the establishment of the Astrophysical Observatory, the National Gallery of Art, and the National Zoological Park.

While at the Smithsonian Institution, Langley continued the experiments with heavier-than-air aircraft that he had begun earlier. The field of aeronautics was ridiculed at the time, and many people, including scientists, thought that humans would never fly. Langley was considered a serious scientist; his peers criticized his studies in aeronautics. From 1891 through 1893, he built and flew 31 propeller-driven model airplanes powered by rubber bands. Some of his model aircraft, which he called "aerodromes," flew distances of over 75 feet.

In 1891, Langley published "Experiments in Aerodynamics" and two years later he published "The Internal Work of the Wind." He incorporated the principles of flight from these two papers into a series of powered model biplanes with 14-foot wingspans. Since there were no lightweight gasoline engines, he built gasoline-heated, flash-boiler steam engines that weighed five pounds per horsepower. In 1891, he predicted that a one-horsepower steam engine weighing 20 pounds could propel a 200-pound airplane at 45 miles per hour, and, furthermore, that "mechanical flight is possible with engines we now possess."

In May 1896, Langley's model no. 5 was catapulted from a houseboat at Quantico on the Potomac River, flew 3,000 feet, and landed without damage. Later that year, model no. 6 had a successful flight of 4,200 feet at 35 miles per hour. In 1898, the Bureau of Ordnance of the War Department appropriated $50,000 for him to design and build an airplane to carry a man aloft.

At the turn of the century, Langley was in his 60s and had a heavy build. He hired an assistant, Charles Manley, to pilot the aircraft. Manley, an engineer, had developed the five-cylinder water-cooled radial engine used to power the manned aircraft. The engine, an advanced design for its time, weighed 125 pounds and generated 52.4 horsepower.

On August 8, 1903, a one-quarter-scale model of the manned aircraft flew 1,000 feet with a smaller engine of similar design. A carpenter at the Smithsonian built the body of the manned machine. Thinly drawn steel tubes were used as structural members because aluminum wasn't yet in use.

On October 8, the full-sized biplane with Manley aboard was catapulted from a houseboat on the Potomac River. Manley wore a cork-lined jacket and was so optimistic that he strapped a compass to his leg to use in finding his way back if he got lost on a lengthy flight. Langley was busy with his responsibilities back at the Smithsonian and wasn't present for the test flight. Manley was headed into a five mile-per-hour wind; however, a part of the aircraft caught on the launching device and the plane was projected downward. It came to rest in 16 feet of water about 150 feet from the houseboat. Manley was unharmed.

The press was merciless. This *New York Times* editorial is representative:

> The ridiculous fiasco which attended the attempt at aerial navigation in the Langley flying machine was not unexpected. The flying machine which will really fly might be evolved by the combined and continuous efforts of mathematicians and mechanicians in from one to 10 million years—provided we can meanwhile eliminate such little drawbacks as the existing relation between weight and strength in inorganic materials. No doubt the problem has its attractions for those it interests, but to ordinary men, it would seem as if the effort might be employed more profitably.

Langley used photographs to evaluate the causes of the failure. The 42-foot wings that provided a wing area of 1,040 square feet were insufficiently braced and showed the strain of attempting to lift the 850-pound load of airplane, engine, and pilot. As suspected at the time of the launch, the main problem was that the launching mechanism snagged the aircraft as it began to take off. Other problems were structural deficiencies and shortcomings with the control mechanisms. With funds almost gone and winter approaching, Langley decided to rebuild the aircraft and try one more test flight.

On December 8, 1903, Langley was present at the second launch of the "Great Aerodrome" from the houseboat on the Potomac. The craft hung up again on the launch rail, and Manley said that "just before the machine was freed from the launching car he felt an extreme swaying motion immediately followed by a tremendous jerk which caused the machine to quiver all over." The support wires connecting the tail and rear wings snapped; the aircraft turned upward and fell backward into the water near the houseboat.

Manley almost drowned. He was pinned under the cockpit, and his cork-lined vest snagged on part of the aircraft. He tore the jacket free, came up under a block of ice, and swam to open water. His frozen clothes had to be cut from him, and he was given a tumbler of whiskey. He wasn't used to drinking; he uttered the "most voluble series of blasphemies" ever heard around the Smithsonian. When asked about this later, Manley had no recollection of it.

Again, the newspapers attacked Langley. One reporter suggested that the aircraft should be sent off the houseboat upside down to improve its chances of getting airborne. The *New York Times* added, "We hope that Prof. Langley will not put his substantial greatness as a scientist in further peril by continuing to waste his time, and the money involved, in further airship experiments. Life is short, and he is capable of services to humanity incomparably greater than can be expected to result from trying to fly." Other columnists called the aircraft a "buzzard" and "Langley's Folly" and accused Langley of wasting public funds.

Langley observed after the December trial: "Failure in the aerodrome [aircraft] itself or its engines there has been none; and it is believed that at the moment of success, and when the engineering problems have been solved, that a lack of means has prevented a continuance of the work." He didn't continue with the aircraft trials. Private individuals, including Jacob Schiff, offered to fund further development work, but Langley refused their support. In his opinion, it was a project from which the nation would benefit, and therefore development support should come from public funds. Unfortunately, the Bureau of Ordnance had lost interest in his experiments.

After deciding not to continue with his aircraft experiments, Langley commented, as cited by John A. Breashear in *The Autobiography of a Man Who Loved the Stars:*

> I have brought to a close the portion of the work which seemed to be specially mine: the demonstration of the practicality of mechanical flight. For the next stage, which is the commercial and practical development of the idea, it is probable that the world may look to others . . . The great universal highway overhead is now soon to be opened.

Many factors were involved in Langley's giving up his aircraft experiments, including health problems, the burden of the administration of the Smithsonian Institution, and being overwhelmed by the adverse comments of the press. Negative comments about his experiments from other members of the scientific community bothered him most of all. An attempt was even made to remove him from his position as secretary of the Smithsonian.

In November 1905, Langley suffered a stroke. He recovered partially but lost the use of his right arm and leg. He suffered a second stroke and died on February 27, 1906. A friend observed that he died "feeling in many ways that his life had been a failure."

Langley wasn't a failure in life. He made significant contributions to the fields of astronomy and aircraft design and was the recipient of many scientific honors, including the gold and silver medals of the American Academy of Arts and Sciences, the gold medal of the National Academy of Sciences, the Janssen medal of the Institute of France, and the Rumford medal of the Royal Society of London.

WILBUR AND ORVILLE WRIGHT—Inventors of the Airplane

"The miracle, the power, that elevates the few is to be found in their industry, application, and perseverance under the promptings of a determined spirit."

Mark Twain

Neither Wilbur nor Orville Wright graduated from high school. Wilbur didn't graduate because their family moved from Indiana to Ohio before he finished his senior year, and Orville took advanced college preparatory courses in his junior year that prevented him from graduating with his class.

Wilbur and Orville excelled in mathematics and science and benefited from growing up in an inquiring, well-educated family. In December 1892, the brothers opened their first shop in Dayton, Ohio, to sell and repair bicycles. In 1895, they began to design and build their own bicycles because of increased competition in selling and repairing bicycles.

Wilbur and Orville worked extremely well as a team; it is unlikely that either would have achieved the success individually that they accomplished together. Wilbur observed that "From the time we were little children my brother Orville and myself lived together, played together, worked together and, in fact, thought together. We usually owned all of our toys in common and talked over our thoughts and aspirations so that nearly everything that was done in our lives has been the result of conversations, suggestions, and discussions between us."

On May 30, 1899, Wilbur wrote to the Smithsonian Institution requesting information about human flight. He wrote that "my observations . . . have . . . convinced me that human flight is possible and practicable." He intended to "begin a systematic study of the subject in preparation for practical work." The Smithsonian recommended "Experiments in Aerodynamics" by Samuel Langley and "Progress in Flying Machines" by Octave Chanute.

To test their ideas about control systems, Wilbur built a small two-winged kite with a wingspan of five feet and a chord (wing width) of 13 inches. They used a canard configuration with the stabilizing surface (elevator) ahead of the wings. With this kite, they tested their concept of "wing warping" that provided control of the craft's roll motion in the air, which, in modern aircraft, is controlled by ailerons in the wings.

In August 1900, Wilbur and Orville started constructing their first full-sized glider capable of manned flight. Wilbur asked Octave Chanute and the National Weather Bureau for recommendations on a site for their test flights. Wilbur selected Kitty Hawk, North Carolina, because of its 15- to 20-mile-an-hour winds, its lack of hills and trees, and its sandy surface.

Wilbur had planned to buy 18-foot lengths of spruce en route for use as spars, but the longest he could find were 16-foot lengths. They modified their kite's wingspan and used a smaller wing surface area than they had planned, 165 square feet instead of 200. Wing chord was five feet. The total weight of the craft was 52 pounds.

In October, the tethered glider flew with a man on board. Their neighbor, young Tom Tate, did most of the piloting because he weighed less than Wilbur or Orville. The brothers also flew the glider as a unmanned kite using lines to the ground to control it. After several days of tests, the glider was caught in a gust of wind and severely damaged. They spent three days repairing it.

On October 20, Wilbur became the first of the brothers to experience free flight. Wilbur conducted flights of 300 to 400 feet over a duration of 15 to 20 seconds. The brothers were disappointed with the lift of the glider, but they realized it was at least partially due to the reduced wing area. After completing the trials, they left for Dayton on October 23 with plans to build another glider at Kitty Hawk the following summer.

The 1901 glider was a biplane with a wingspan of 22 feet, a chord of seven feet, and a wing area of 290 square feet. The camber (curvature) of the wing was increased. The 98-pound craft was the largest flown up until that time. In Dayton, they hired a machinist, Charlie Taylor, who later designed and built the engine for their 1903 aircraft. In July 1901, Wilbur and Orville again traveled to Kitty Hawk.

Wilbur conducted the test flights. The lift and the speed of the new glider were disappointing. Control of pitch wasn't as responsive as they had hoped, and Wilbur experienced a few stalls in which the forward stabilizer assisted him in making a safe landing. In August, Wilbur made flights of 13 seconds or more over distances of up to 389 feet.

The wing warping mechanism worked well, but they experienced a reversal in the roll motion of the glider that they couldn't explain. On one flight, Wilbur was distracted when this occurred, and he didn't respond quickly to the controls. He dropped onto the sand abruptly and suffered a black eye and a bruised nose. Soon afterward, they returned to Dayton. On the way back to Dayton, Wilbur told Orville that "men would not fly for 50 years."

Charlie Taylor, whose assistance was essential to their experiments, designed and manufactured their first internal combustion engine. With a machinist like Taylor, the Wrights were now able to make airplane parts of increased complexity.

Wilbur and Orville built a small wind tunnel to use in checking the coefficients required to design their aircraft. It wasn't the first wind tunnel, but the discipline they used to apply aerodynamic data directly to the design of aircraft was new. They collected data for a variety of wing configurations to use in lift and drag formulae. They also studied the aspect ratio, the ratio of the wingspan to the wing chord. The brothers learned that long, narrow wings produce more lift than short, wide wings with the same wing area. In December, they discontinued their experiments and returned to the bicycle business that financed them.

Wilbur and Orville designed the 1902 glider with a wingspan of 32 feet and a wing chord of five feet (compared with the 1901 wingspan of 22 feet and a chord of seven feet) that doubled the aspect ratio. In February 1902, they added a fixed rudder to address the problem of the reversal of the direction of a roll when the wing warping mechanism was applied.

Wilbur and Orville returned to Kitty Hawk and on September 19, the 1902 glider with 305 square feet of wing area was ready for its first test. It had a forward elevator of 15 square feet and a longer, narrower rudder than the 1901 glider. The new glider weighed almost 120 pounds. The first tests were unmanned; they made 50 tests covering distances of under 200 feet during the first two days.

In the first manned flights, Wilbur encountered crosswinds that affected the lateral stability more severely than on previous models. Orville began to make flights at this point. On one of his early attempts, he lost control at an altitude of 30 feet with disastrous results for the glider. Fortunately, Orville was unhurt. It took them three days to rebuild the craft.

The reversal of the roll motion when the wing warping mechanism was applied, the cause of Orville's crash, was a recurring problem. In the middle of the night, Orville thought of a solution to the problem. In the morning, he suggested to Wilbur that they install a movable rudder to compensate for the sudden change in direction. Wilbur suggested that the rudder control be coupled with the wing warping mechanism because the pilot already had enough on his mind. The evolution of the controls of the Wright airplane was now complete. Three-axis motion could now be controlled; that is, they could control pitch, roll, and yaw. They had invented the first truly controllable aircraft and were ready for powered flight. On October 28, they left for Dayton.

During the winter, Wilbur and Orville designed the 1903 powered aircraft that they called the "Flyer." They calculated that the airplane would weigh 625 pounds with a pilot, assuming that the propellers and engine weighed 200 pounds. No commercially available four-cycle engine met their specifications of eight or nine horsepower with a weight of under 180 pounds. Charlie Taylor designed a 12-horsepower engine with four cast-iron cylinders in a cast-aluminum crankcase cooled by a water jacket. It had no radiator or water pump; the water didn't circulate.

The Wrights used bicycle sprocket and chain technology to connect two contra-rotating pusher propellers mounted behind the wings with the engine. The 1903 craft had a wingspan of 44 and 1/3 feet, a 6 1/2-foot chord, and a wing area of 510 square feet.

In September 1903, the Wrights left for Kitty Hawk. For three months, they experienced bad weather, many technical problems, and some disappointing flights with the 1902 glider. The loaded weight of the 1903 aircraft had increased from 625 to 700 pounds.

Wilbur won the coin toss to fly the plane on its first lift-off from a 60-foot-long launching rail. The "Flyer" lifted off the rail at the 40-foot point, reached an altitude of 15 feet, stalled, and dropped onto the sand, damaging the forward elevator and one of the skids. This 3 1/2 second flight of 100 feet wasn't considered a real flight.

On December 17, the temperature was freezing and the wind was blowing at 27 miles per hour. It was Orville's turn to pilot the airplane; the brothers shook hands as though they weren't going to see each other again. At 10:35 a.m., the "Flyer" lifted off after traveling about 40 feet on the rail and flew 120 feet in 12 seconds.

This flight was considered the first true flight. Orville commented, "The flight lasted only 12 seconds, but it was nevertheless the first in the history of the world in which a machine carrying a man had raised itself by its own power into the air in full flight, had sailed forward without a reduction in speed, and had finally landed at a point as high as that from which it started."

Wilbur flew the second flight of the day over a distance of 175 feet, followed by Orville in a flight of over 200 feet that lasted 15 seconds. Wilbur flew the "Flyer" on the last flight of the day—a flight of 852 feet with a duration of 59 seconds. While they were discussing the flights, a gust of wind overturned the "Flyer," breaking spars, struts, most of the wing ribs, and the engine crankcase. No more flights were conducted in 1903. However, the Wright brothers had accomplished their goal; they had pioneered powered flight.

In 1904 and 1905, the brothers built two more powered aircraft to continue their experiments. They moved their test flights from Kitty Hawk to Huffman Prairie, eight miles from Dayton. The success of the last 1903 flight wasn't matched until the 49th flight in 1904. On September 20, 1904, they made their first circular flight, which lasted 96 seconds and covered 4,080 feet. On October 5, 1905, Wilbur circled the field 30 times in 39 minutes, spanning a distance of 24 1/2 miles.

In 1908 and 1909, the brothers successfully marketed their aircraft in the United States and Europe through sales and licensing agreements. In 1910, they established the Wright Company for manufacturing aircraft, conducting exhibitions, and training pilots. Orville ran the company while Wilbur fought the patent infringement suits. Weakened by the strain of the legal process, Wilbur died on May 30, 1912, four weeks after contracting typhoid fever.

Orville brought the suits to successful conclusion in 1914. He sold his interests in the Wright Company in 1915 and retired a wealthy man. Orville lived a long, quiet life in retirement. He suffered a heart attack and died on January 27, 1948.

* * *

The approaches taken to developing the first heavier-than-air aircraft by Samuel Langley and by Wilbur and Orville Wright could not have contrasted more sharply. Langley was more of a scientist than an inventor. As the secretary of the Smithsonian Institution in Washington, D.C., he had many interests other than developing the first successful airplane.

Although Langley conducted many tests with rubber-band powered models, he conducted few tests with full-sized aircraft. He pinned all of his hopes on two manned test flights conducted from a houseboat on the Potomac River in full view of spectators, newsmen, and photographers. His principal problem was the launch mechanism, not the aircraft, although the craft also had structural shortcomings and control limitations. Langley was in his 60s at the time of his 1903 test flights; he hired a pilot to test fly the airplane for him. Langley wasn't even present at his first manned test flight.

In contrast, Wilbur and Orville Wright were hands-on inventors with years of experience in bicycle design, manufacturing, and maintenance. They had their own machine shop. Their investigation of the principles of aerodynamics was ongoing and extremely focused.

All of Wilbur's and Orville's focus was on applied development that improved the design and manufacture of a manned craft that could fly. They devoted virtually all of their time for four years to that goal. Although they had to work in their Dayton bicycle shop during the winter season, they devoted their lives to their aviation project.

The Wright brothers conducted a large number of early test flights, including flying their gliders unmanned as kites. Their experiments were conducted in the solitude of the sand dunes in Kitty Hawk, North Carolina, away from newsmen, photographers, and spectators. The brothers worked out of the limelight. They piloted their own aircraft.

The source of funding was another major difference between the efforts of Langley and the Wright brothers. Langley's work was funded by the War Department because of the potential use of aircraft for aerial reconnaissance. Theodore Roosevelt, Assistant Secretary of the Navy, helped Langley obtain a grant for $50,000.

The Wright brothers paid for all of their development work themselves with earnings from their successful bicycle manufacturing and maintenance shop in Dayton.

Another key difference between Langley's development and the Wright Brothers' was the environment within which they functioned. Langley had a network of scientific colleagues, but they thought that he was wasting his time and effort developing aircraft. In fact, they suggested that he drop the effort because he was damaging his reputation as a serious scientist. Langley's pilot was an employee, the designer of his engine, which was superior to the Wright engine—particularly the power to weight ratio.

The Wright brothers, on the other hand, had each other. If one of them didn't think of a good solution to a problem, the other one did. One brother would originate an idea; the other brother would improve upon it or enhance it. The Wright family and friends were very supportive of their effort.

Langley, by doing his experimentation in public, became the target of many jibes and critical newspapers articles. The abuse that he received in the newspapers bothered him. He was a respected scientist; he wasn't thick-skinned. Eventually, the controversy surrounding his experiments affected his health. After the two unsuccessful manned flights and the withdrawal of government funding, Langley dropped his effort to develop a manned aircraft because he believed it should be a national effort, not an individual effort.

The Wright brothers, by conducting their work in seclusion, were never a target of the press as Langley was. Their focused determination, coupled with a willingness to make incremental improvements to modify their designs to incorporate the findings of their test flights, were key ingredients in the ultimate achievement of their goal.

Unfortunately, Langley discontinued his work when he was on the threshold of success. Fortunately, the Wright brothers persevered and launched the aviation age.

EPILOGUE

Improving Emotional Intelligence

"The most exciting and promising aspect of Emotional Intelligence is that we are able to change it. In other words, unlike our IQ, we are not stuck with what we are born with. The great news about EQ is that it is not fixed or only developed at a certain stage of life. It has been shown that life experiences can be used to increase our EQ and that we can continue to develop our capacity to learn and adapt as we grow older. The EQ realm is one area that does reward us for successfully having gone through stages of our lives."

Harvey Deutschendorf, *The Other Kind of Smart*

The place to begin in increasing one's Emotional Intelligence is self-awareness, knowing oneself, particularly strengths and weaknesses. A positive self-regard is important. We should stay positive, even when discussing our weaknesses. For example, if someone asks about our impatience, we can admit to being impatient but that we are working on it, and it is getting better.

In choosing the area to begin with in increasing your Emotional Intelligence, pick the area in which you have the most to gain. Improvement cannot be expected to occur overnight. For many people, working on controlling their impulses, not saying the first thing that comes to their minds, will come first.

In *People Smart,* Mel Goldman has listed skills that can be worked on and improved, including:

- Expressing Yourself Clearly—get the message across
- Asserting Your Needs—be straightforward but establish limits
- Exchanging Feedback—be descriptive without giving offense
- Influencing Others—be able to motivate others
- Resolving Conflict—define problems and suggest solutions
- Being a Team Player—build consensus
- Shifting Gears—be flexible and resilient

In *Emotional Intelligence Works,* S. Michael Kravitz and Susan D. Schubert list skills that can more fully developed, including:

- Improve Your Listening Skills
- Adapt to the Communication Needs of Others
- [Learn How to] Confront Negative People
- Develop Social Skills
- Foster Optimism
- Encourage Flexibility and Problem Solving
- Model and Encourage Emotional Control
- Support Teamwork

Extroverts tend to have more people smarts than introverts. Nevertheless, we can all improve our people skills. Self-assessment surveys can be helpful in establishing the starting point of our efforts to improve our Emotional Intelligence.

In 1980, Reuven Bar-On developed a test to measure Emotional Intelligence. The BarOnEQ-i, or Emotional Quotient Inventory, has been approved by the American Psychological Association.

In 1990, John Mayer, Peter Salovey, and David Caruso developed the Mayer-Salovey-Caruso Emotional Intelligence Test (MSCEIT). It is an ability-based test of Emotional Intelligence.

These tests may be helpful in a program to increase Emotional Intelligence. Anyone desiring to improve his or her chances of achieving success will be motivated to spend the time and the effort.

As stated earlier, a purpose of this book is to provide role models of Emotional Intelligence from history from whom we can learn skills to aid in increasing our EQ. For a more comprehensive discussion of Emotional Intelligence and how to increase EQ, works by authors quoted in this book are highly recommended.

What Constitutes Success

"To laugh often and much, to win the respect of intelligent people and affection of children; to earn the appreciation of honest critics and endure the betrayal of false friends; to appreciate beauty; to find the best in others; to leave the world a bit better, whether by a healthy child, a garden patch, or a redeemed social condition; to know even one life has breathed easier because you have lived. This is to have succeeded."

Ralph Waldo Emerson

BIBLIOGRAPHY

Andrews, Linda Wasner. *Emotional Intelligence*. New York: Franklin Watts, 2004.

Aronson, Marc. *Up Close: Bill Gates*. New York: Viking, 2009.

Bar-On, Reuven, J.G. Maree, and Maurice Jesse Elias, editors, *Educating People to Be Emotionally Intelligent*. Westport, CT: Praeger, 2007.

Barry, Kathleen. *Susan B. Anthony: A Biography of a Singular Feminist*. New York: New York University Press, 1988.

Blegen, Carl W. *Troy and the Trojans*. New York: Barnes and Noble, 1995.

Boyd, Thomas. *Poor John Fitch, Inventor of the Steamboat*. New York: Putnam's, 1935.

Branden, Nathaniel. *Six Pillars of Self-Esteem*. New York: Bantam, 1994.

Breashear, John A. *The Autobiography of a Man Who Loved the Stars*. New York: American Society of Mechanical Engineers, 1924.

Bronfield, Jerry. *Rockne: The Man, the Coach, the Legend*. New York: Random House, 1976.

Brown, Jordan. *Elizabeth Blackwell*. New York: Chelsea House, 1989.

Burlingame, Roger. *Out of Silence into Sound: The Life of Alexander Graham Bell*. New York: Macmillan, 1964.

Burns, James McGregor. *Roosevelt: The Lion and the Fox*. New York: Harcourt, Brace, 1956.

Casper, Christine Mockler. *From Now On with Passion: A Guide to Emotional Intelligence*. New York: Cypress House, 2001.

Chambers, Peggy. *A Doctor Alone, A Biography of Elizabeth Blackwell: The First Woman Doctor 1821-1910*. London: Abelard-Schuman, 1958.

Coles, Robert. *Dorothy Day: A Radical Devotion*. Reading, MA: Addison-Wesley, 1987.

Coolidge, Olivia. *The Apprenticeship of Abraham Lincoln*. New York: Charles Scribner's Sons, 1974.

Cooper, Robert K., and Ayman Sawaf. *Executive EQ: Emotional Intelligence in Leadership and Organizations*. New York: Grosset / Putnam, 1997.

Cousins, Margaret. *The Story of Thomas Alva Edison*. New York: Random House, 1965.

Crouch, Tom D. *The Bishop's Boys: A Life of Wilbur and Orville Wright*. New York: Norton, 1989.

Curie, Eve. *Madame Curie*. New York: Doubleday, 1930.

Cushnir, Raphael. *The One Thing Holding You Back: Unleashing the Power of Emotional Connection*. New York: Harper One, 2008.

Day, Dorothy. *Loaves and Fishes*. Maryknoll, NY: Orbis Books, 1963.

—. *The Long Loneliness: The Autobiography of Dorothy Day.* San Francisco: Harper Collins, 1952.

Deutschendorf, Harvey. *The Other Kind of Smart*. New York: Amacom, 2009.

Deutschman, Alan. *The Second Coming of Steve Jobs*. New York: Broadway Books, 2000.

Douglass, Frederick. *The Life and Times of Frederick Douglass*. New York: Thomas Y. Crowell, 1956.

Egan, Eileen. *Such a Vision of the Street: Mother Teresa—The Spirit and the Work*. Garden City, NY: Doubleday, 1985.

Fischer, Louis. *Gandhi: His life and Message for the World*. New York: New American Library, 1954.

Gardner, Howard. *Multiple Intelligences: The Theory in Practice*. New York: Basic Books, 1993.

Goleman, Daniel. *Emotional Intelligence: Why It Can Matter More Than IQ*. New York: Bantam Books, 1995.

—.*Working with Emotional Intelligence*. New York: Bantam Books, 1998.

Gordy, Wilbur F. *Abraham Lincoln*. New York: Scribner's Sons, 1918.

Gray, Charlottte. *Mother Teresa: Her Mission to Serve God by Caring for the Poor.* Milwaukee: Garrett Stevens, 1988.

Griffith, Elizabeth. *In Her Own Right: The Life of Elizabeth Cady Stanton*. New York: Oxford University Press, 1984.

Hamilton, Leni. *Clara Barton: Founder, American Red Cross*. New York: Chelsea House, 1988.

Hancock, Thomas. *Personal Narrative of the Origin and Progress of the Caoutchouc or India Rubber Manufacture in England.* London: Longman, Brown, Longmans, & Roberts, 1857.

Heller, Robert. *Bill Gates: Genius of the Software Revolution*. New York: Dorling Kindersley, 2000.

Honour, Alan. *The Unlikely Hero: Heinrich Schliemann's Quest for Troy*. New York: McGraw-Hill, 1960.

Hubbard, Elbert. *Elbert Hubbard's Scrapbook*. N.p., Wm. Wise & Co., 1923.

Hylander, C. J. *American Inventors*. New York: Macmillan, 1958.

Jakoubek, Robert. *Martin Luther King, Jr.,* New York: Chelsea House, 1989.

Keller, Helen. *The Story of My Life*. New York: Airmont Books, 1965.

Keller, Mollie. *Winston Churchill*. New York: Franklin Watts, 1984.

Kelly, Fred C. *The Wright Brothers*. New York: Harcourt Brace, 1943.

Klees, Emerson. *The Drive to Succeed: Role Models of Motivation*. Rochester, NY: Cameo Press, 2002.

— . *Entrepreneurs in History—Success vs. Failure: Entrepreneurial Role Models*. Rochester, NY: Cameo Press, 1995.

—. *People of the Finger Lakes Region*. Rochester, NY: Friends of the Finger Lakes Publishing, 1995.

—. *Staying With It: Role Models of Perseverance*. Rochester, NY: Cameo Press, 1999.

—. *The Will To Stay With It: Role Models of Determination*. Rochester, NY: Cameo Press, 2002.

Kravitz, S. Michael, and Susan D. Schubert. *Emotional Intelligence Works: Developing People Smart Strategies*. Menlo Park, CA: Crisp Learning, 2000.

Maslow, Abraham H. *Motivation and Personality*. New York: Harper & Row, 1970.

Matthews, Gerald, Moshe Zeidner, and Robert D. Roberts. *Emotional Intelligence: Science and Myth*. Cambridge, MA: MIT Press, 2002.

Miller, Douglas T., *Frederick Douglass and the Fight for Freedom*. New York: Facts on File, 1988.

Miller, William D. *Dorothy Day: A Biography*. San Francisco: Harper & Row, 1982.

Philip, Cynthia Owen. *Robert Fulton: A Biography*. New York: Franklin Watts, 1985.

Richards, Norman. *Dreamers and Doers*. New York: Antheneum, 1984.

Rogers, William. *THINK: A Biography of the Watsons and IBM*. New York: Stein and Day, 1969.

Ross, Ishbel. *Child of Destiny: The Life Story of the First Woman Doctor*. New York: Harper & Brothers, 1949.

Sebba, Anne. *Mother Teresa: Beyond the Image*. New York: Doubleday, 1997.

Segal, Jeanne. *Raising Your Emotional Intelligence: A Practical Guide*. New York: Henry Holt, 1997.

Seligman, Martin E. P. *Learned Optimism*. New York: Alfred A. Knopf, 1991.

Silberman, Mel. *People Smart*. San Francisco: Berrett-Koehler, 2000.

Stein, Steven J., and Howard E. Book. *The EQ Edge: Emotional Intelligence and Your Success*. Toronto, Canada: John Wiley & Sons, 1996.

Strachey, Lytton. *Eminent Victorians*. New York: Harcourt Brace Jovanovich, 1918.

Thompson, Sylvanus P. *Philipp Reis: Inventor of the Telephone*. London: Spon, 1883.

Traill, David A. *Schliemann of Troy*. New York: St. Martin's Press, 1995.

Wallace, Francis. *Knute Rockne*. Garden City: NY: Doubleday, 1960.

Wallace, James, and Jim Erickson. *Hard Drive: Bill Gates and the Making of the Microsoft Empire*. New York: Harper, 1992.

Weisinger, Hendrie. *Emotional Intelligence at Work: The Untapped Edge for Success*. San Francisco: Jossey-Bass, 1998.

Wilson, A. N. *The Life of John Milton*. New York: Oxford University Press, 1983.

Wilson, Susan. *Steve Jobs: Wizard of Apple Computer.* Berkeley Heights, NJ: Enslow, 2001.

Woodruff, William. *The Rise of the British Rubber Industry During the Nineteenth Century*. Liverpool: Liverpool University Press, 1958.

Zeidner, Moshe, Gerald Matthews, and Richard D. Booth. *What We Know about Emotional Intelligence*. Cambridge, MA: MIT Press, 2009.